GROUP PROCESS

GROUP PROCESS

Working Effectively by Committee

Robert K. Laber, Ed.D

TECHNOMIC
PUBLISHING CO., INC.

LANCASTER · BASEL

Group Process

aTECHNOMIC ᵏpublication

Published in the Western Hemisphere by
Technomic Publishing Company, Inc.
851 New Holland Avenue, Box 3535
Lancaster, Pennsylvania 17604 U.S.A.

Distributed in the Rest of the World by
Technomic Publishing AG
Missionsstrasse 44
CH-4055 Basel, Switzerland

Printed in the United States of America
10 9 8 7 6 5 4 3 2 1

Main entry under title:
   Group Process: Working Effectively by Committee

A Technomic Publishing Company book
Bibliography: p.
Includes index p. 87

Library of Congress Catalog Card No. 96-61886
ISBN No. 1-56676-501-3

*To my wife, Donna, for all those evenings alone
while I was out meeting with committees*

CONTENTS

"EVERYONE ALTERS AND is altered by everyone else," wrote Gerald Brenan in *Thoughts of a Dry Season* (1978). "We are all the time taking in portions of one another or else reacting against them, and by these involuntary acquisitions and repulsions modifying our natures."

In *Working Effectively by Committee,* Robert Laber focuses on both the vehicle and instrument of change: the committee. By their very construct and nature, as Laber observes, committees have styles; they have personalities; they have maturational growth; they have meaning. They are living, breathing organisms which grow and change as do the members who participate within them. And, like anything organic, they observe a set of natural processes, axioms and laws.

In a quasi-Maslow-like construct, Laber sets the stage for understanding the interaction of processes and people by taking the reader from the very definition of a committee through the complexities of organizations, planning and conflict resolution. Focusing on the seminal idea that process is as important as product for organizations, Laber focuses on the human dimension, from the singularity of the individual's role on a committee to the Burnsian notion that committee leadership is both "transactional and transformational." It is a reach that is broad, yet surprisingly focused.

In his book, *The Fifth Discipline,* Peter Senge (1993) speaks about this notion that organizations have to be "broadly defined yet clearly focused." He cites ten characteristics of "learning organizations" which must be in place for organizations to move, grow and change:

(1) Assess your learning culture.
(2) Promote the positive.
(3) Make the environment safe for thinking.
(4) Reward risk-taking.
(5) Help people be resources for each other.

(6) Put learning power to work.

(7) Map out a vision.

(8) Bring the vision to life.

(9) Connect the systems.

(10) Get the show on the road.

Committees, as Laber aptly illustrates, are really learning organizations. They have cultures; they need to deal with negative behaviors to make the environment safe for thinking; they need to resolve conflict to reward risk-taking; they need organization and planning to put learning power to work; they have to have strong leadership to map out a vision; and they have to be synergistic to connect all the systems and move forward to bring the vision to life. *Working Effectively by Committee* is a perfect example of how committees play an integral role in the Sengian notion of learning organizations.

Change, however, does not come easily to any organization. The author is fully cognizant of this axiom throughout the book, but addresses the issue head on in the final section of the book on the "planner's tool kit." It is here that we receive the tools—specific, rudimentary, and focused—so that the committee, and its leadership, can meet its charge. In fact, it is this section which very much parallels the thinking of Michael Fullan in his book *Change Forces* (1993). Fullan's notion of educational reform is that for a new paradigm of change to occur, eight basic lessons for dynamic change must be learned:

Lesson 1: You can't mandate what matters.
Lesson 2: Change is a journey, not a blueprint.
Lesson 3: Problems are our friends.
Lesson 4: Vision and strategic planning come later.
Lesson 5: Individualism and collectivism must have equal power.
Lesson 6: Neither centralization nor decentralization works.
Lesson 7: Connection with the wider environment is critical.
Lesson 8: Every person is a change agent.

Laber's understanding of the workings of a committee closely parallel these eight lessons. And, just as the notions of the committee as a learning organization are strongly prevalent, so too is the notion of the committee as change agent.

In understanding the full impact of *Working Effectively by Committee,* we arrive at what Pascal in *Pensees* (1670) recounted: "It is not certain that everything is uncertain." Robert Laber has demonstrated that working with committees—as living organisms, as learning organizations, as change agents has elements that demonstrate certainty. It is the clarity of his melody throughout which enables us to understand how committees can be put to work effectively and successfully for organizational decision making. *Working Effectively by Committees* is a must read for everyone who wants to use committees effectively.

JONATHAN T. HUGHES, PH.D.
Associate Professor
Dowling College
October, 1996

THIS YEAR ALONE, thousands of Americans, and thousands more worldwide, will participate in committees. Many of these participants will take on leadership responsibility for committees of one kind or another. And while most prospective chairs have thought about what they would like their committees to accomplish, few have probably examined, to any degree, the committee process itself.

What makes some committees effective? Why do others miss their mark? Why do some people chair committees with style and grace, while others simply officiate over a hopeless morass of tedious personality conflicts? The answer, in part, is cultural. Most of us have learned how to run committees from our participation on other committees—at first hand with both positive and negative models. Committees, after all, have a tendency to operate the way they always have in the past. Meeting style is a part of every organization's culture, whether it is a corporation, school, government or non-profit agency, or a department, civic group, church or synagogue committee, club board, or neighborhood association.

Yet, there is a science to the operation of committees, and an art to how they may be managed productively and effectively. This is a book on the *art of committee*—a guide to what to do and what to expect. It is about the art of managing the interaction of people and ideas, about giving shape to life; it is about observation and intuition, conflict management, organization and preparedness; it is about the art of working with others to accomplish goals, and about doing all of this with style—the craft and the art of committee.

This book has been designed to both inform and to lead. It addresses both the theory and practice of committee organization and management. In Chapter 1, we will look at the structure of committees: how large they should be to accomplish what kinds of tasks, together with the role and organization of subcommittees. We will examine the concept of synergism—how the whole becomes more than the sum of its parts.

Chapter 2 focuses on individuals in groups. We will look at "styles of representation," group dynamics, and how the behaviors, maturity levels, and motivations of individuals tend to interact in the group process.

Chapter 3 is an examination of the basic work unit of the committee, the meeting. We will look at why meetings are held, then examine the six basic types, and how they differ in purpose, structure, and operation. Chapter 3 also looks at the dynamics of meetings and the inner mechanics of meeting operation. We will look at the consensus building process and the behavior obstacles that commonly impede it, and observe the importance of a ground rules statement and its importance in meeting control.

Chapter 4 moves on to address meeting and committee organization, including an overview of why meetings and committees most commonly fail. This chapter provides a series of tools—sample committee and meeting organizers to assist the chair in the step-by-step planning and evaluation of successful, well-organized, and professionally executed committee work.

The final chapter looks at the all-important role of leadership: the role and responsibilities of the chair or committee/meeting facilitator. Chapter 5 examines the principles of effective interaction, identifying negative or obstructionist behaviors and ways to deal with them expediently and skillfully. Practical, easy to master conflict management techniques and the unique principles and operational techniques of the "interactive meeting" are explored—all to the end of informing and nurturing the leadership process, the art of committee.

CHAPTER 1

Sizes, Structures, and Synergism—How the Whole Becomes More Than Its Parts

A COMMITTEE, ACCORDING to *New American Webster's,* is simply "a body appointed for specific duties"—illustrating that brevity is sometimes the soul of under-explanation. Committees are often called by other names: commissions, delegations, panels, boards, councils, task teams, and in some parts of the world, juntas. Committees are often referred to in less than flattering terms. Humorist Fred Allen was particularly cutting in his definition: "A committee is a gathering of important people who singly can do nothing, but together can decide that nothing can be done." British scientist Barnett Cocks was clearly not a great believer in committees. He described them as: "Cul-de-sacs down which ideas are lured and then quietly strangled." But, committees remain *the* mechanisms by which organizations make decisions. And in today's world, when big decisions are to be made, they will most likely be made by—or with the help of—some kind of committee.

In business, committees are used to pool skills and resources, identify issues, divide up work, and provide a vehicle through which information can be quickly communicated as participants bounce ideas off each other. A committee is used when it is necessary to collectively size up a situation or problem and come up with an organizational response. Committees are used to insulate individuals when difficult decisions have to be made. And, they provide a venue for the young and "on the rise" to show their stuff—or lack of it.

In government and education, committees are used to address nearly all important policy and planning issues—not only for the same reasons businesses use them (above), but for idea flotation: testing responses to various options from various constituencies before making them public. Committees also play a central role in public sector management because representation in the decision-making process is so vital—a prerequisite to successful implementation of practically every new plan or idea. Of course, in the world of politics and government, there is another impor-

1

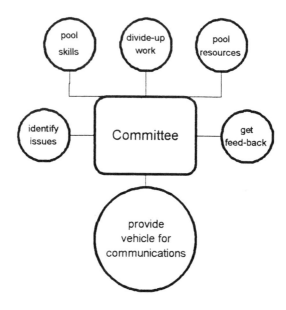

tant reason. If "a camel is a horse designed by a committee," it was probably a government committee, convened because no individual wanted to be publicly identified with so potentially controversial a decision. Yes, like it or not, organizations run on committees; they cannot effectively function without them. Certainly there is a body of research and lore on the science of organizing and operating committees. I'll impart some of this as we go along. What is more important, however, is understanding that real committee leadership is an art, and that the skills of the chair or facilitator are key.

French artist and writer Jean Cocteau defined art as "a marriage of the conscious and the unconscious." This is the essence of successful committee leadership: bringing what is expressed and observed into alignment with what is sensed and understood. Even the most skillful chairperson or facilitator cannot rely on scientific management procedures alone to provide the subtle adjustments that will bring a committee to genuine consensus; but he or she can "feel the moment," if attuned to the behavior cues of the participants. Playwright Jean Anouilh, a compatriot of Cocteau, expressed it another way: "The object of art is to give shape to life." Committees are animate objects that, once brought into being, take on a life of their own. Giving shape to this life is the art of committee.

COMMITTEE SIZE

How Big Should a Committee Be?

Well, how many people does it take to have a good party? The answer to both questions is basically the same: it depends on the chemistry of the group. The research, however, supports that to deal with questions that are fundamentally technical or strategic in nature, a committee of about six—certainly not more than seven or eight—is optimal. This size enables informal, free flowing meetings that can be managed effectively and reach decisions efficiently; but there is a down side. A small committee may not have the expertise, experience, and knowledge necessary to arrive at a well-considered decision on every aspect of the issue at hand. There is another danger. Small committees that make decisions tend to consist of a manager or hierarchical leader and a collection of subordinates. Such groups often have a rubber-stamp mentality, particularly if the leader writes the performance reviews of the rest of the group, or if the chair, even subtly, suggests that agreement with him or her is expected. There is another problem called *Groupthink,* a kind of organizational tunnel vision. It occurs when members of a tight

---

On The Lookout For Groupthink

When an idea is put forward,

- is there thoughtful, critical discussion of its ramifications?

- does someone serve as "devil's advocate" to point out possible problems with the idea?

- are alternatives suggested?

- are the solutions, options, or suggestions really different?

- is a suggestion examined from the perspectives of other constituencies and groups, including those that are affected by it?

- is proof or "back-up" requested and provided to support statements?

```
How To Tell If
Your Committee
Is too Small
```

■   The participants do
    not have the knowledge
    and/ or experience
    necessary to fully
    understand the issue
    at hand.

■   The participants are
    not sufficiently rep-
    resentative.

■   The options or sug-
    gestions coming from
    committee participants
    are not sufficiently
    varied or rich.

little "in" group are so accustomed to working with each other that they think the same way. They look at others in unrealistic, often stereotypical terms, and believe so strongly in their own superiority or morality that other perspectives are not sufficiently considered. Such a group tends to construct rationalizations rather than real solutions, and the group exerts a kind of peer pressure on its members to avoid deviating from what appears to be the group consensus. Ironically, *Groupthink* usually afflicts bodies that have made successful decisions in the past. The group is *so* confident, it has been lulled into complacency and a sense of omnipotence.

There is another problem. Just because a committee—even a top-level, high-powered committee—makes a decision, it does not necessarily follow that everyone else will think the decision is a good one. This is true, though perhaps not voiced, even in highly autocratic, hierarchical organizations, despite Lyndon Johnson's observation to the effect that "when you've got them by the ears, their hearts and minds will follow."

Yet small, efficient committees are best for making decisions that are strategic or technical in nature; they are essential when decisions involve confidentiality or controlling access to information. They are also good for planning, organizing, or executing work, including the work of coordinating larger, more broad-based committees. But when a committee has the task of making decisions that will require the participation of others for successful implementation, a larger group is usually required because representation in the decision-making process becomes a key factor.

About eight to fifteen or sixteen participants are typically needed for a committee that will allow for representation, diversity of viewpoint, and/or richness of knowledge or expertise. This is the ideal size for committees that establish action plans. If the matter of representation has been carefully accommodated in forming the committee, a group of this size can produce decisions that can be effectively thought out and smoothly implemented. A mid-size committee of six to fifteen is small enough to operate efficiently and informally, although its meetings require planning and structure. It is large enough for the effective use of interactive techniques. (These will be discussed in Chapter 5.) On the negative side, the mid-size committee requires greater organization and management from the chair. And, where time is money, the larger committee requires taking more people away from what they normally do for a longer time.

Finally there is the "monster" committee. This is a committee of twenty to thirty people. Such a committee can be very difficult and frustrating to lead. Its chairperson or facilitator needs a great deal more than a whip and a chair to bring consensus out of a group this big, but a little bit of negative experience can be an extremely effective teacher. First, there are obstacles to manage, even before the first meeting is called to order. Monster committees can be brutal to schedule, particularly if they are made up of volunteers. Then there is the "who not to invite" dilemma. Clearly, the prime reason to establish a monster committee is to provide broader representation in the decision-making process. So, the members of such a committee must be acknowledged, credible representatives of, or spokespersons for, some particular constituency or organizational subgroup. This is where big egos come into play. The relative rank of the delegates must be carefully considered. Normally, it is best to let the sending organization or subgroup determine who their representative(s) will be, but even this will probably take some give and take. It is vitally important to sort this out before the first meeting takes place. Bruised egos back at the sending group can undermine a committee's work.

There is also the problem of establishing the tone and feel of the committee's all important first few meetings. Where to hold big meetings is also important. The place must be reasonably convenient, attractive, and set up in advance. The location should *say* that the meeting has importance by being held in an important, well-appointed place. But be aware of whose turf it's on; neutral ground is usually best. Furniture and seating arrangements are important details. Don't reinforce or enable established cliques; divide these people up. If participants are unlikely to know each other, preprinted nameplates and badges are a must. Hospitality arrangements need to be planned: coffee, fruit, and pastries, etc., tend to lower anxieties. By all means, never make people pay for parking.

In short, everything about the welcoming and opening of a "monster" meeting must be pleasant, relaxed, amicable, carefully planned, and above all respectful—even when some of the members have displayed in the past that they deserve a whole lot less. But these are only the basics; the topic of meeting planning will be addressed more systematically in Chapter 4.

However, there are some important strategic considerations associated with effectively managing large committees, and these are pertinent to this overview. Participants in monster committees do not, at first, have the sense that they are participating as individuals. They are there to represent an interest or provide a particular kind of expertise. Cliques can be present or develop quickly, and the chairperson or facilitator needs to get some wedges into these before they develop into solidified coalitions. Coalitions are just like cliques except more so; they are better organized and there is usually some kind of common bond, or common enemy, holding them together. Large meetings must be structured, ground rules must be established, and a system for letting everyone speak is necessary. While this is not an environment where creative problem solving can easily occur, interactional techniques (discussed in Chapter 5) can be used effectively by an experienced facilitator. Even with these negatives, the monster meeting, handled skillfully, can be a beautiful sight to behold. Its big plus is broad-based representation at the meetings, so when such a committee successfully arrives at consensus decisions, implementation can usually occur smoothly and quickly, communication beyond the committee is facilitated, and the committee's decisions will tend to have a high degree of credibility. But large committees depend upon a highly skilled chair or facilitator. They depend upon preparation, organization, and the effective use of subcommittees.

SUBCOMMITTEES

Subcommittees are small, working groups that report back to the full committee. Figuring out what these subcommittees should be, who should be on them, and how much autonomy they should have depends upon the persuasive power of the chair or facilitator and the consent of the full committee. Individual members of large committees tend to have their own agendas and not much identification with the large committee. Participants will more likely develop bonds with small subcommittees. For this reason, it is usually better to have several small subcommittees rather than one or two larger ones. Keeping the work of subcommittees narrow in scope and compressed in duration will enable the chair to have more of them, and rotate their membership. The process of subcommittees reporting back to the full committee builds esprit and a sense of progress. Subcommittees are vital to whittling a big committee down to a manageable size, but there is a caveat. Members of large committees often do not feel responsible for making them work, so the chair or facilitator must not disperse the committee into work groups too soon. Timing in this decision, as in most of life, is everything. Much of the timing depends on the individual committee members' style of representation. (We will look at style of representation in Chapter 2, along with other participant behavioral characteristics. These conceptual frameworks from the behavioral sciences are extremely important and deserve their own space and separate discussion.)

When Is a Committee Too Large?

Theoretically, committees of more than thirty or so are possible through application of the basic monster committee principles discussed above. But as a rule of thumb, meetings of more than thirty people are probably managed best through some form of parliamentary procedure. Research, at least, supports this contention.

SYNERGISM

What merits further consideration is how committees can be structured to work *synergistically*. Synergism is achieved when the whole becomes more than the sum of its parts. First, let's look at the notion of coordinated or interlocking committees.

Synergism through Coordination

It is obvious that where multiple committees have been organized to address well-defined parts of one huge task, some kind of oversight or *coordinating committee* is essential. Complex undertakings like a military invasion, a corporate headquarters move, or a school district reorganization require steering committees to make sure all of the pieces are complete and that they fit into proper sequence. What is less apparent is that even committees working on seemingly unrelated projects also need to be coordinated. Committees working in isolation can easily develop recommendations, decisions, or action plans that, if carried out, would get in each other's way or even work counterproductively. What results is an unhealthy competition among committees, unnecessary competition for resources and management commitment, and worst of all, organizational confusion. In the public sector, where committee reports are often presented publicly, lack of coordination also results in public confusion, and this can have all kinds of negative repercussions. Unfor-

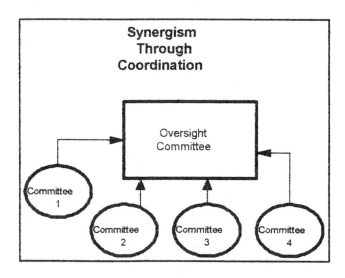

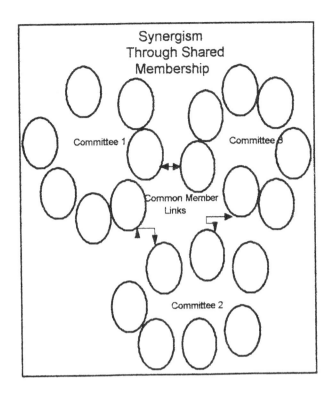

Synergism
Through Shared
Membership

Committee 1

Committee 3

Common Member
Links

Committee 2

tunately, we see this all the time at the federal, state, and local levels of government, and at all levels of public education. Actually, with a few simple, reasonable steps this kind of chaos can be easily avoided. First, as in major organizational projects, management needs an oversight committee. This committee should be small. It should include a few top-level managers and either the chairperson or another representative from each of the other committees. The function of the oversight committee should be to provide a forum for communication and coordination. Its job is not to tell the other committees what to do or to serve as a watchdog. Regular briefings by committee chairs will inform other committees and identify where coordination can, or should, occur. When one committee understands where another may be headed, coordination becomes possible, and the progress and work of one committee can stimulate the others.

Shared membership is another way committees can be interlocked for communication and coordination purposes. When one committee shares a member or two with another committee, a communication link is formed. But this only functions if the individuals involved understand that they have this special role. It should be part of their responsibility to keep each committee abreast of permanent developments, decisions, recommendations, or problems that are occurring in other committees.

Synergism through Teams

Teams are not committees and committees are not necessarily teams. Now that that's perfectly clear, let me add that these two animals, when encountered in the wild, can look very much alike; the distinctions, however, are important. Today, many top American corporations, following the lead of Japanese industry, are resolutely going about the business of forming cross-functional teams. Rather than try to define this term, let me give an example. At the Xerox corporation, the regional sales manager, area operations manager, and service manager all function together as a team, which has the authority and responsibility for running its own relatively autonomous operation. What is new in this model is that the local sales manager, instead of reporting vertically to a sales hierarchy, is responsible to his or her team. The same thing is true of the operations manager and the service manager. In effect, these individuals are operating a little company, which is ultimately responsible to the big company. Even the corporation's bonus structure is predicated upon the degree to which the team has achieved its goals; the fate of everyone on the team is tied, first and foremost, to the team's results. The team is said to be "cross-functional" because individuals responsible for the sales, operations, and service functions of the business, in a geographic territory, are the members of the team.

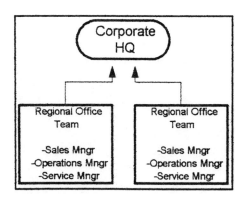

In their comprehensive text on the subject, *The Wisdom of Teams: Creating the High-Performance Organization,* authors Jon Katzenbach and Douglas Smith illustrate through case studies the thinking that underlies such a model: the principle is that teams must develop complementary skills—all of the technical and functional expertise, problem solving and decision making, and interpersonal skills necessary to achieve the team's goals. The authors' definition of a team, in this context, is as follows: "a small number of people with complementary skills who are committed to a common purpose, performance goals, and approach for which they hold themselves mutually accountable."[1] What sets the tone and dictates the priorities for such a team is one major thing: a well-articulated and understood common purpose. The purpose gives the team "an identity that reaches beyond the sum of the individuals involved."[2] There is a teamwork product; specified, compelling performance outcomes are targeted by the team. As identified by Katzenbach and Smith, the dynamic power of the "team" is that as goals are discussed and the approaches to them developed, the people involved—over time—have a clearer and clearer choice: they can disagree with the goal and the path the team selects and, in effect, opt out of the team; or they can pitch in and become jointly accountable with their teammates. The team, therefore *is* the primary operational unit within which everything else takes place. So, without belaboring the point, teams, as they are now being developed in American industry, are like committees on steroids. What is most important in the context of our examination of committees is how synergism is achieved through this team model. Committees can, in fact, take on team-like characteristics for certain periods of time in non-team types of organizations; they can operate within the existing organization but on a more intermittent basis. The "all for one" factor is not built into a committee's group work ethic as it is in a team. But can cross-functional teams operate within broader organizations? Katzenbach and Smith say yes, explaining that "sizeable groups can function as extended teams whose performance is stimulated well beyond what one would expect in a hierarchy because of the influence of a real team in their midst."[3]

It is the performance goals accepted by a team that challenge—actu-

---

[1]Katzenbach, Jon R. and Smith, Douglas. *The Wisdom of Teams.* Boston: Harvard Business School Press, 1993, p. 45.
[2]See footnote 1.
[3]See footnote 2.

ally, compel—the team's members to make a difference. Unlike most committees, it is this "drama, urgency, and healthy fear of failure that combine to drive teams who have their collective eye on an attainable goal."[4]

This quest to achieve synergism, by one means or another, is part of the broader canvass that embodies the art of committee.

[4]Katzenbach, Jon R. and Smith, Douglas. *The Wisdom of Teams.* Boston: Harvard Business School Press, 1993, p. 55.

CHAPTER 2

Individuals in Groups

INTUITION AND OBSERVATION are key elements of the art of committee. But conceptual frameworks from the behavioral sciences enable explanation and interpretation of the human behavior that intuition and observation only identify.

STYLES OF REPRESENTATION

"Man," Aristotle postulated in the 4th century B.C., "is by nature a political animal." And so it follows that men and women bring an inherently "political" nature with them when they serve on committees. Oh, people might not think they're political, but on committees, just about everyone represents some other interest, some ideology, or something when they take part in a committee. As Aristotle phrased it, "All that we do is done with an eye to something else." How a committee participant perceives the interests of whomever and whatever he or she represents is the essence of the decision-making process; how the participant approaches the decision-making process is his or her style of representation.

In his 1976 book, *The Politics of Administrative Representation,* political scientist Dale Mann identified three fundamental styles of representation: trustee, delegate, and politico. A trustee style of representation is one in which individuals, in this case committee participants, perceive themselves to be acting on behalf of their constituents. Trustees are those that tend to vote their own minds on an issue. This, they perceive, is why they are on the committee. Trustees are those who will be most persuaded by facts and reason. Interestingly, trustee-style representatives will usually make decisions based on what they perceive to be the needs and interests of their constituents or clients, even when those decisions run counter to the expressed opinions or demands of the constituents or clients themselves. This is because the trustee feels he or she knows what is best; he or she is the one who has studied the issue and is in possession of the facts. Delegates are just the opposite.

The delegate style of representation is one in which individual committee members are guided by the expressed preferences of their constituents, even when these preferences contradict their own judgment. Delegates are usually those individuals who perceive they are on a committee to represent the views of a particular faction in relation to another faction(s): minority groups versus a majority group; clearly defined but opposing ideologies (liberals versus conservatives); power groups (representatives from unions versus representatives from management, or manufacturing versus sales); interest groups (those that are in power versus those that aren't); economic factions (the haves versus the have-nots); or social factions (the "haves" versus the "have-mores"). Delegates require very special handling by a committee chair or facilitator. Since delegates believe they must respond to their constituency by

---

Preparation Exercise

1. *Know Your Own, Fundamental Representation Style*

Trustee	Delegate	Politico
You obtain relevant facts and make decisions on the basis of what you believe is the logical course of action.	You obtain relevant facts and make decisions on the basis of what those whom you represent want to happen.	You obtain relevant facts and evaluate them within the context of the political situation at hand.

2. *Recall a number of decisions you have made or influenced in a variety of situations. Over time, which of the above models best characterizes your fundamental approach to these decisions?*

3. *Which of the above decisionmaking models do you believe would serve you best in the role of: (a) committee chair, (b) subcommittee chair, (c) committee member? Why?*

giving it what it says it wants, delegates cannot compromise easily. Neither can they become too enamored with facts or reasons not in their interest. They often feel great pressure to suppress or even misrepresent facts and others' statements. Delegates can experience a good deal of inner conflict over decisions, and more often than not end up clinging to familiar rhetoric or carping about "the inadequacy of the process." So, the chair or committee facilitator must stay on the alert for common ground, ways for delegates to save face, and eventually ways in which extreme positions can come to a perceived win-win, or if all else fails, lose-lose consensus.

The politico style of representation is in many respects the most interesting to watch. Committee chairs and facilitators have to be politicos to some degree. The politico members of a committee are those who are ultimately the most useful to the committee since they keep the process moving. The politicos are the deal makers and the power brokers. A politico responds to some issues as a delegate and to others as a trustee, but in a consistent way. The choice is more than simple vacillation. A politico reads a situation, then determines, often intuitively, whether to respond in a delegate or trustee style. The politico is also a compromiser; the politico will find the common ground and come up with a position that will work. But while the politicos are the lifeblood of a committee, the chair or facilitator cannot allow them to operate too freely. And, there should not be too many politicos on a committee. A meeting of politicos would be an empty ceremony. With neither passion nor sense of mission beyond the urgency of the situation, politicos, by themselves, are tools without purpose.

LEVELS OF MATURITY

Another important body of behavioral theory concerns what Kohlberg and other psychologists have identified as stages of moral development. In the same way that individual committee members bring with them their "representation style," each individual also comes with a certain level of maturity as an adult, a person's characteristic level of maturity. An individual's level of maturity determines how he or she can see and think through a decision.

Theoretically, each adult's level of maturity can be categorized into the following six stages:

- Stage 6: Integrated
- Stage 5: Autonomous
- Stage 4: Conscientious
- Stage 3: Conformist
- Stage 2: Self-Protective
- Stage 1: Impulsive

At the lowest level, someone operating at the *Impulsive* stage is characterized by self-centeredness. Such an individual tends to see only his or her own point of view. Work is done for direct reward, not usually for any higher purpose. This is the "what's in it for me" type of individual who has an entirely egocentric frame of reference. Such an individual is immature, and to convince him or her to support a certain decision, he or she must be shown how the decision directly serves his or her interests.

At Stage 2, the *Self-Protective* level, the individual accepts only limited responsibility, has little capacity for creativity or abstraction, and must be given continuous, concrete direction. An individual at this level has limited capacity for effective cooperation, will not venture an independent opinion, and will not normally risk disagreeing except to avoid taking chances.

At the *Conformist* level, Stage 3, the individual blindly follows rules, procedures, and established policies; he or she does and says what is expected to avoid negative reinforcement, not because of any real understanding of why the rules, procedures, or policies have been established in the first place. On a committee, this is an individual who will distrust outsiders and will be thrown off-balance by almost any deviation from established conventions. Individuals at the conformist stage of development will tend to take direction from and follow the lead of others they perceive to be in authority.

At the *Conscientious* level, Stage 4, the individual has an inner moral sense and a concern for the overall. He or she has a sense of obligation and responsibility. This individual has ideals and a sense of inner responsibility to do what is "right," but is not yet fully in touch with his or her inner feelings. This is a person who often shows initiative, but who does not yet have a fully developed sense of personal identity, and may tend to be overly self-critical and unsure of him or herself when wisdom and inner strength are needed.

At the *Autonomous* level, Stage 5, individuals are tolerant and have a well-developed moral framework, but are concerned primarily with their own individuality and self-fulfillment. Such individuals are aware of

```
Preparation Exercise
When you make decisions, what is
typically foremost in your thinking?

What's in it for me?    Impulsive
_____
What is the safest
decision?               Self-Protective
_____
What do those in
authority expect me     Conformist
to do?
_____
What is my responsi-
bility in this situ-    Conscientious
ation?
_____
What do I want to
see happen?             Autonomous
_____
What, in the big
picture, is the right
decision given all the  Integrated
facts and responsibili-
ties involved?
```

their inner conflicts and of conflicting duties and loyalties. While they are open-minded and respectful of the views and opinions of others, they are independent and often ambivalent and indecisive in dealing with issues and decisions.

Stage 6 is the *Integrated* level. Individuals at this stage of maturity, or moral development, have a strong sense of personal identity. With this level of maturity comes a superior perception of reality and an increased acceptance of oneself and others. Individuals at the integrated stage have an increased capacity to give, to see the big picture, and to form a perception that is not self-centered, but expansive, wise, and accepting.

GROUP DYNAMICS

Beyond the constructs of "style of representation" and "stage of maturity" discussed above, there is a whole behavioral science that has grown up around how people conduct themselves in groups; it's the study of group dynamics. Different writers and psychologists have identified and categorized the common "behavior types" one encounters in group meetings. While actual labels differ, the basic behavior types tend to be similar from study to study, depending on the specific kind of organization being examined. Having been active throughout my own career in educational and community organizations, arts councils, and a handful of corporate and government bureau advisory boards, I've empirically developed my own descriptors; I call them the Five Cs: *chargers, chatterers, champions, compromisers,* and *contemplators.*

The Charger

This is the kind of committee member who is aggressive, confident, and assertive. Chargers are quick to put forth a position and quick to attack another's. Chargers can be delegates or trustees—not normally politicos unless they are "performing" for calculated effect. As delegates, chargers are aggressive because they perceive they have a position to defend or attack. As trustees, chargers tend to be the vigorous interrogators, but delegates also attack through interrogation to put an opponent on the defensive. A well-prepared, experienced charger can easily take control of or destroy a committee unless kept in check by the chair or meeting facilitator.

The Chatterer

Chatterers are, as the name implies, those committee participants who take up a disproportionate amount of committee air time with sometimes aimless, often irrelevant comments and storytelling. However, their importance to committee dynamics should not be underestimated. Chatterers are often politicos who are just a bit nervous, intimidated, or otherwise ill at ease. They provide a vital function in stimulating conversation and helping in the early stages of getting committee meetings off the ground. They are also the people who break tension when it arises, and who often have something very important to say. Chatterers can be instrumental in helping a committee achieve consensus on a given issue. But like chargers, unless kept under control by the chair or meeting facilitator, chatterers can destroy a committee. Any seriously constituted committee has a right to expect the chair to keep the chatterer under control. In addition, no committee should have to suffer a charger who is also a chatterer.

The Champion

The champion is like the charger except for an important distinction. While the charger's excess is aggressiveness, the champion's is passion. Champions tend to be emotional and assertive; they feel strongly about certain causes or positions and sincerely feel themselves to be putting forth or defending what is "right." Champions can be either trustees or delegates, but they are rarely politicos. When consensus is finally reached by a committee, the champions have the potential for being the committee's most enthusiastic or unenthusiastic spokespersons.

The Compromiser

The compromiser is a pure politico. Since compromisers tend to get along well with the other participants, they are the individuals who maintain good working relations with those on both sides of an issue, and who can be the most instrumental in achieving consensus. Every good committee needs one or two good compromisers. However, compromisers are politicos, and as such, do not always show their true stripes until absolutely necessary. Compromisers often masquerade as trustees and sometimes even delegates. They tend to be very shrewd individuals who will find areas of agreement between chargers, champions, and contemplators, without ever putting themselves in the middle of the debate. While compromisers are useful committee workers, they do not usually believe strongly in the issues, and have the capacity to be satisfied with a committee decision or product that is inadequate but expedient.

The Contemplator

Everyone likes to think of him or herself as one of the "thinkers" or "seers" on a committee. But the real contemplators are those who speak very little, then all of a sudden jump in with a truly insightful observation or remark. Or, they may have to be drawn out. Contemplators deal in facts but often care deeply, though not overtly, about the issues. They generally enjoy the respect of the committee's participants, and though usually trustee in orientation, can turn out to be very effective politicos. However, people may not always be what they seem, and a participant who looks and acts like a contemplator can turn out to be someone else's stooge, or worse, someone who simply doesn't have anything intelligent to contribute.

When committees work well, the above categories will generally suffice to characterize the way participants behave. But, these behaviors are relative—sometimes blatant and sometimes subtle. And, people sometimes modify their behavior as a committee deals with different issues. A champion on one issue might be a contemplator on another. But over time, each individual will tend to demonstrate a characteristic representation style and behavior mode. In corporations and other "closed" organizations where someone, perhaps even the chair, is in a position to control the formation of a committee, problem participants can be screened out. However, in other arenas such as government and education, the chair occasionally must work with unknown commodities—often individuals elected or recommended by a sending organization. In these cases the chair or facilitator may find him or herself working with an expanded pallet of behavioral types, besides the occasional out and out "provocateur." Sometimes committee meetings do not go well, or some individual perceives that the committee is moving in an "unacceptable" direction. This can give rise to two aberrant behavior types.

The Dissenter

This is the individual who either pouts or overtly displays negative behavior; makes negative, disparaging, or sarcastic comments; or ends up raising "process" issues with the chair, objecting to the way decisions were reached or that the debate has been cut off. The dissenter will usually be a delegate but could be a trustee. Sometimes, a dissenter is also a charger or a champion who has not gotten his or her way.

Preparation Exercise

What kind of committee member do you tend to be in most situations?

Charger, Chatterer, Champion, Compromiser, or Contemplator

What are the statements a committee chair might make to you to control your behavior, when necessary, without hurting your feelings?

Generally, the dissenter is best dealt with privately—one-on-one by the chair or facilitator. Some good humor and understanding from the chair can bring the dissenter back on board. Sometimes opportunities exist to allow the dissenter to be redirected into a subcommittee chairmanship or given another assignment that will allow him or her to continue to contribute to the work of the committee in a way that is mutually perceived as important. Sometimes the dissenter might choose to resign, but if he or she has been elected or invited to the committee to represent some interest, the chair should work to keep the member involved.

The Deserter

In other instances, a committee participant—maybe even a dissenter—will simply disengage from the meeting, cease participation, and either pout, doodle, or show no interest. This is another situation that generally is best dealt with privately, one-on-one, by the chair or facilitator because sometimes the withdrawal has been caused by some minor misunderstanding. A deserter might be a chatterer who has been rebuked insensitively. An apparent deserter could be a contemplator who is thinking, a compromiser waiting for his or her moment, or a charger or champion who has not prevailed in his or her efforts. Whatever the reason, a deserter is a distraction to small- and mid-size committees, so it is important that this kind of behavior be addressed quickly and sensitively by the chair. As with the dissenter, opportunities should be sought or developed to redirect the deserter into some committee function that will be mutually perceived as important.

In addition to the above, there are three additional, though happily less prevalent, types of committee participants. There are some individuals who become involved in committees who simply do not belong there. I refer to them as transients, and there are two basic types.

Transient A

The first kind of transient is the individual who habitually misses meetings. In some situations the participation of this individual is so important to the committee's work that his or her attendance pattern simply has to be overlooked. However, in most cases, the person who regularly misses meetings should either be replaced or simply disregarded. For one thing, a meeting truant endangers the discipline and morale of the committee, and the chair should not be terribly gracious in tolerating this behavior or it will quickly spread. Personally, I have rarely taken more than five seconds of committee time to update an individual who regularly misses meetings, unless there is a very good reason for this pattern. In addition, meeting missers can slow the momentum of a committee if they have any important role to play in the committee's work. Consequently, a suspected Transient A should not be given anything important to do unless there is a very strong reason to believe that the increased responsibility will modify the behavior.

Transient B

The second form of transient is the individual who is so inconsistent or unfocused that he or she just has to be politely disregarded from the standpoint of group dynamics. Unlike the chatterer, who has a role to play in the group, a Transient B has no real dynamic function to offer the committee except, in the public sector, to represent, however inadequately, whatever or whomever he or she is supposed to represent. These individuals tend to vacillate between delegate, trustee, and politico styles of representation, sometimes out of confusion. They are normally not bothered in the least by inconsistent and idiosyncratic behavior in themselves or others. In business organizations, this kind of individual is not usually tolerated. In the public sector at least, these are often political people who are just off on their own trip. If amicable, a Transient B can be an amusing individual, who does not impede the progress of the committee significantly. At the worst, a Transient B can become a loose cannon who operates outside the parameters of the committee. In either case, it usually pays to find some way to replace this kind of transient.

The Official

There is another type of dynamic which can affect a committee—one that is external to the process. It involves another kind of transient who is generally overlooked in studies of group process. It is the appearance of what I will call the *official*. Male or female, the official is a high organizational officer, maybe the individual to whom the committee will report; maybe the general manager, mayor, president, superintendent, or chair of the board. The official might even be serving as an *ex-officio* member of the committee. This is the individual who drops in on a committee meeting "just to keep in touch." A visit from an official is a major event in group dynamics. The visit usually has strategic importance, and can either be very helpful or very destructive. The official can be an information resource and sounding board. He or she can stimulate progress by giving encouragement and confirmation that the committee's work is heading in an acceptable direction. Enthusiasm from this individual can spur the committee to work all the harder. A visit from the official can also be used to confirm the authority of the committee chair or facilitator, and smoothly bring an out-of-control charger or champion into line.

There are also times when committees stall or reach impasses that cannot be easily resolved. Depending on the issues, circumstances, and personalities, the official can sometimes be helpful in redirecting and/or re-energizing a floundering committee. But a visit from the official can also destroy a committee or leave its chair with nothing but pieces to reassemble. First, the official should not enter into the committee as a participant. This upsets the normal dynamics of the group, sometimes changing them irrevocably. Second, the official should not countermand or otherwise undermine decisions tentatively reached by the group. It is normally enough for him or her to politely identify points of conflict with organizational direction or policy. And third, the official should not visit a committee too often. Frequent visits to a committee from officialdom tend to undermine the committee's confidence in its chair or facilitator. The presence of an official also distorts the normal dynamics of the group and thereby destroys its autonomy and consensus building capacity. A committee works best when it is left alone to grapple with its own issues in its own way.

The foregoing conceptual frameworks (representation style, levels of maturity, and the study of group dynamics) are tools that a committee chair, facilitator, or participant can use to help explain why people on committees behave the way they do. However, it is only in the actual committee arena itself—the meeting—that behaviors become dynamic; therefore, it is in the management of these behaviors that we witness the art of committee.

CHAPTER 3

The Meeting: Work Unit of the Committee

HAVING CONSIDERED THE factors of representation style, participant maturity level, and group dynamics, we now come to the basic work unit of the committee, the meeting. Author/psychologist Myron Gordon[5] developed a good, simple definition: "A meeting is a structured and planned situation where people work together in a give-and-take relationship to do one or more of the following:

- expedite decisions
- evaluate
- present and share
- create and explore
- teach and train
- solve problems"

Committee meetings are convened for a variety of purposes, and can be structured differently to accomplish different tasks—sometimes by the same group at different times. Described here are the most common types of meetings.

EXECUTIVE COMMITTEE MEETINGS

Executive committee meetings are advisory in nature. The leader convenes the meeting, presents the issue under consideration and asks for committee input. Participants discuss the issue, pointing out alternatives and the pros and cons associated with each position. The leader then makes the decision.

[5]Gordon, Myron. *How to Plan & Conduct a Successful Meeting.* New York: Sterling Publishing Co., 1981.

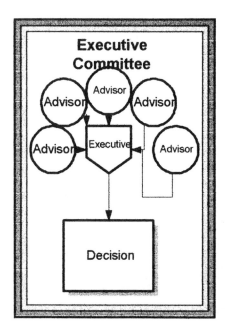

RESOURCE COMMITTEE MEETINGS

Resource committee meetings are those at which the leader makes a final decision based on the advice of individuals on the committee who are the most knowledgeable, experienced, or *expert* on the issues at hand.

INFORMATION PRESENTATION MEETINGS

Information presentation meetings are normally structured, highly linear meetings at which someone presents information, which is then discussed. The meetings are run by the chair, who moves through an agenda; the chair either presents the information or introduces the presenter(s), and loosely manages the discussion portion of the meeting. At the end, the chair summarizes or "ties off" the discussion—ideally showing how the information or presentation will be used by the committee and relates any future course of action suggested by the presentation, the discussion, or both.

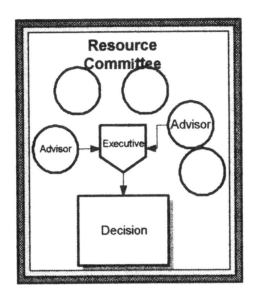

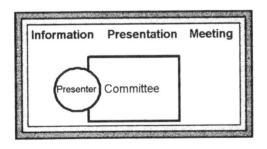

CREATIVE COMMITTEE MEETINGS

Creative committee meetings are typically free flowing meetings that require little actual direction from the chair. In fact, such meetings might not make use of a chair, in the traditional sense. A different kind of meeting leader, called a facilitator, might be employed instead.

Authors Michael Doyle and David Straus[6] define the role of meeting facilitator as "a meeting chauffeur, a servant of the group." The facilitator is not an authority figure. "Neutral and non-evaluating, the facilitator is responsible for making sure the participants are using the most effective methods for accomplishing their task in the shortest time." The facilitator runs the meeting and takes the participants where they need to go, but is not otherwise a participant in the process. In a creative meeting, the task of the chair or facilitator is to define the objective or problem, and through the committee process, search for new combinations of ap-

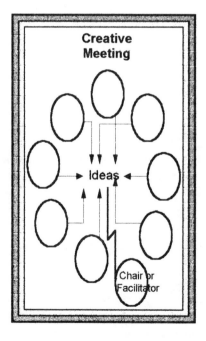

[6]Doyle, Michael and Straus, David. *How to Make Meetings Work.* New York: Jove Books, 1982.

proaches, thoughts, solutions, and ideas. Brainstorming is typically used in creative meetings.

Brainstorming

The purpose of brainstorming is to break down the floodgates and release the full force of the participants' ideas—one person's imagination stimulating another's. In a successful brainstorming session, no suggestion is discouraged, no matter how farfetched or outlandish. The whole purpose is to call forth the greatest possible richness and breadth of participant responses. Often the facilitator must prod the group to keep momentum and individual imagination flowing. Speed is important; individuals can be encouraged to yell out—not speak in any particular order, but the facilitator must try to draw everyone out. All ideas must be recorded quickly (as they flow out), on a large tablet of paper or blackboard where they can be seen by the whole committee. In the second phase of brainstorming, the committee steps back, looks at all of their ideas, and—through the leadership of the facilitator—begins to cluster them into groups of ideas that are variations on each other. In step three, the committee then focuses on the clusters of ideas that seem to be the most promising. The facilitator then organizes the remainder of the session to begin examining any or all clusters the committee wishes to consider, analyze, or develop; members elaborate and question, and through this process, begin to more clearly define and shape the ideas that were generated by the group.

The brainstorming activity is a valuable technique in almost any kind of committee, but particularly those with a creative task, because it allows some ideas to emerge and survive that would not otherwise. People usually find it easy to find problems with an idea—particularly one that is truly fresh and untried. The brainstorming process puts that idea in play and keeps it there for future consideration.

Brainstorming also serves as a means of focusing the committee. Brainstorming has important "process" functions. It is an ice breaker for a new committee; it tends to break down the inhibitions of participants because it sweeps them up in the momentum of what is, in effect, a group game. It encourages and builds teamwork. It also gives individual participants a chance to shine and demonstrate their personal creativity, imagination, and intelligence.

At the later stages of the brainstorming exercise, when individual ideas or clusters are examined and evaluated by the individual participants, the alert, perceptive facilitator (or chair) gets valuable insight into the positions of each member who offers a comment or opinion.

TEACHING AND TRAINING MEETINGS

These kinds of meetings normally are not used for committee work unless the committee needs to "learn" something before dealing with related issues. Teaching and training meetings are like classes except that they commonly involve more small group work as part of the model. For these meetings the presenter has a plan—a curriculum containing the subject matter to be taught, sequenced in a logical, step-by-step way. The curriculum is presented at the predetermined knowledge level(s) of the session participants. The curriculum is presented, ideally, in a variety of teaching modes: *visually* through pictures, charts, graphs, or words; *aurally* through the leader's verbal presentation; *experientially,* through small group discussions and application of the information to sample problems or situations: and *indirectly,* through assigned readings and

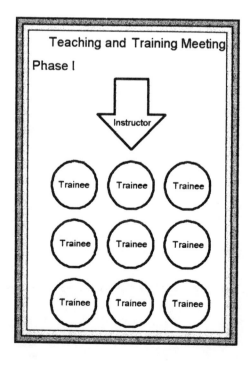

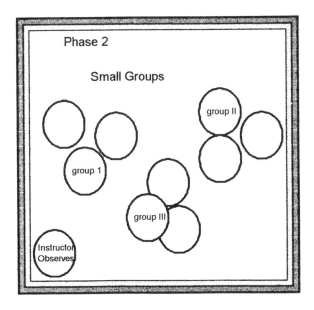

follow-up examinations or small group discussions. Training and instruction are supported through practice, review, and reinforcement.

COMMITTEE PROBLEM-SOLVING MEETINGS

These meetings generally follow a series of steps and are, therefore, highly structured. The job of the chair is to keep the process moving and to keep the steps in order. The usual steps are as follows:

(1) Problem or task is defined.
(2) Relevant data and other pieces of information are examined and discussed by the committee.
(3) Options are developed.
(4) Criteria for evaluation of the options are determined and applied.
(5) Options are analyzed with additional supporting data.
(6) Conclusions or recommendations are made.

CONSENSUS VS. DEMOCRATIC PROCESS

When meetings deal with matters that are purely technical—unencumbered by complex, external considerations—the appropriate mix of

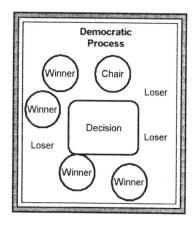

expertise, experience, and judgment is assembled around the table, the steps are carried out, and the problem is addressed. Sometimes, however, the kinds of issues that are dealt with by committees are complex and require a process designed to select among options. There are two major ways this is done: through the *democratic process* or through the *consensus building process.*

While the "majority will" concept is generally perceived as fair, it does create winners and losers instead of a cohesive group that ultimately supports the decision in some agreed-upon ways. Both expedient and efficient, a decision arrived at through democratic means can also be a decision that has not been adequately examined, discussed, understood, or defended. It is sometimes just a railroaded decision achieved by a voting coalition. However, democratic process is really the only practical way to make decisions when working with committees of more than about thirty people. With smaller groups, consensus building can more readily be achieved.

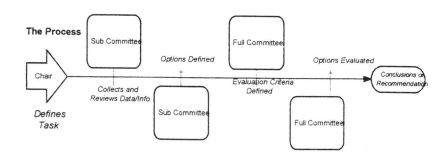

```
┌─────────────────────────────────┐
│           Practice              │
│ When making a decision          │
│ with others, keep               │
│ discussion going until          │
│ each individual expresses       │
│ support for the group's         │
│ decision in some way.           │
└─────────────────────────────────┘
```

A variation on the "majority rules" idea occurs when the leader does not actually call for a vote, but selects what he or she perceives to be the popular position, then refers to it as a "consensus" because people don't always understand what the consensus process actually involves.

Consensus is both a means and an end. Defined formally as "general agreement as to opinion," consensus has come to mean *the position that most or all of the participants can live with.* The consensus building process requires that *all* group members participate openly: experience, share, argue, sense, feel, analyze, synthesize, apply, experiment, and evaluate relevant ideas, beliefs, data, and opinions to form reasoned conclusions and recommendations through agreement. All members must feel they have had a chance to express their views, and to say they will support the committee's decision(s), though they may have reservations. A consensus is neither a unanimous decision nor a majority decision arrived at through formal vote. It is an expressed position that most of the committee's members can support as reasonable, fair, and/or the best option under the circumstances. Though characteristically time-consuming, difficult, and frustrating for everyone involved, consensus building meetings are, in the end, a most effective way to address or resolve complex issues and develop decisions that will help win support for implementation. But meeting management is key.

Consensus Building Meetings

In *How to Plan & Conduct a Successful Meeting,* author Myron Gordon suggests that, to work effectively, consensus building meetings involve the following fundamental activities:

- experimenting
- weeding
- cultivating

In my own experience, *experimenting,* encompasses the following kinds of activities: the introducing, broadening, heightening, deepening,

Practice
At your next problem solving meeting, get the group to go through these steps (without necessarily telling them in advance what they are doing).

1. Discuss a variety of approaches or possible solutions to the problem (Experimenting).

2. Eliminate those ideas that are unrealistic or unnecessarily complicated (Weeding).

3. Pull out the best of the ideas and develop them with the committee. Maintain a process that supports positive idea development and constructive working relationships (Cultivating)

and comparing of ideas. Experimenting is introducing new possibilities through brainstorming. When a participant implies there is more to an issue than meets the eye, he or she is actually widening the issue. That's experimenting! Illustrating and broadening a point through comparison, metaphor, and other imagery is also experimenting. Experimenting is deepening committee understanding through insight or other abstractions. Experimenting can also include expanding through disagreement, or when necessary, confronting the opinions and conclusions of other committee participants. Experimenting might even include uncovering another participant's motives or behavior to remove blockages and open better channels of committee communication and understanding.

Weeding is the process through which committees eliminate or modify comments, ideas, observations, etc. It is the process of sifting out the irrelevant, the impractical, the unreasonable, the unrealistic, or the unacceptable. Weeding can be both negative and positive. It is negative when participants minimize one another's comments, but positive when they respectfully disagree, argue about what the data say, or constructively try to restrict or refocus conversation, thereby preventing the meeting from wandering off the topic into a maze of unrealistic divertissements. Weeding is also being carried out when the chair or a participant shows that a change of pace, change of direction, or re-direction is needed to focus the committee on its primary task.

Cultivating occurs when committee participants initiate by themselves; respond thoughtfully and factually; encourage and support one another; share experience, knowledge, and data; relate to the task directly; work toward the achievement of consensus; relate to others through language and non-verbal cues; connect and link with previous speakers; and ultimately share personal doubts, second thoughts, or dilemmas about the committee's decisions. As Gordon says, cultivating behavior is that which expedites the pace and direction of a meeting along a steady path. But there are certain behaviors by individual meeting participants that tend to obstruct these constructive committee processes. The major ones are discussed below.

OBSTRUCTIVE BEHAVIORS

Dominating

It is typically the chargers and champions who exhibit this behavior, because to dominate is instinctively their strategy of choice. Dominating is a common strategy employed by delegates because control of how issues are defined is critical; delegates usually have very little flexibility with which to argue their point of view. But dominating can also suggest a psychological need for some participant(s). The need to control or

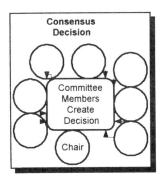

"show-off" is characteristic of a low level of adult development (imma-turity). The chair or facilitator must look deeper, or at least further, before deciding why dominating behavior is being exhibited. The chair could substitute another form of recognition to meet the need of the immature individual, thereby taking him or her out of the way of progress. But in most other cases the key to channeling the charger or champion more productively is to broaden participation—open the arena and draw out all participants quickly; this is an essential tactic. When a committee participant is set upon controlling, he or she shows an unwillingness to work with others' ideas, stifles creativity and debate, and is not open enough to other points of view for consensus building to occur.

Adjudicating

This term describes the kind of behavior in which one is quick to pass judgment on the thoughts and beliefs of others. The participant who is an adjudicator is one who is not readily inclined to consider other points of view or explore alternative approaches or suggestions. Again, this is behavior that tends to be most characteristic of chargers and champions, and most commonly those participants with a delegate style of repre-sentation. However, adjudicating is trustee behavior when an individual participant, who believes he or she knows the facts, simply dismisses another's viewpoint. The chair can fall easily into this negative behavior if not on guard against it. The adjudicator not only inhibits the committee process, but discourages the participation of other members. The unac-ceptableness of this behavior is best addressed up front through the leader's explanation of the committee's ground rules.

CONSTRUCTING GROUND RULES

A way for the chair or meeting facilitator to preempt (to some degree) obstructive behaviors and attitudes is to identify them as unacceptable, and counterproductive in an opening statement. The following is a sample ground rules statement:

As most of you already know, there are certain ground rules which must be established at the outset of any effective committee operation: that everyone has something important to contribute; that everyone has a right to his or her opinions and beliefs; that everyone deserves to have his or her ideas or point of view taken seriously, respected, and considered with an open mind; that everyone must feel free to express his or her own views; and that everyone must participate, contribute, and express an opinion or view on what is at hand.

Evading

Committees sometimes have members who appear to be working constructively with others and who seem to enjoy an easy sense of belonging, but who, when difficult decisions are to be made, will show themselves to be, above all, trouble avoiders. Evaders are usually delegates who find themselves in the uncomfortable position of being isolated from their constituency by the facts of the issue, or the compelling nature of another's rebuttal. More often, however, evasion tends to be a maturity issue. Evaders can be individuals who are self-protective or conformist in their level of development. Evaders are often those who tend to shoulder less than their fair share of responsibility, particularly when decisions become potentially controversial or require difficult choices. Evaders tend to hide behind the committee, and in the consensus building process, try to abstain from difficult decisions for one excuse or another—sometimes posing as contemplators trying to make up their minds. The chair or facilitator must draw these individuals out, help them to make their decision(s), and support them as they become an active voice in the consensus.

Manipulating

Individuals who are devious or inordinately preoccupied with self-interest fall naturally into this kind of behavior. Politicos are often manipulators who masquerade as trustee-contemplators because they are not usually spontaneous and forthcoming (unless the situation requires otherwise). Manipulators can also be instigators and skilled provocateurs who get others to do their bidding. A manipulator is often bright, experienced, and knowledgeable. He or she could be functioning at almost any stage of development (high or low) but usually cannot be taken at face value; there is always some new intrigue in the making.

OBSTRUCTIONIST ATTITUDES

In addition, committee participants may bring counterproductive attitudes that impede constructive group processes. Here are some of the most destructive but most recognizable negative attitudes one regularly encounters on committees.

Superiority

We have all encountered the individual who feels superior to others, either intellectually or in terms of professional or social status. The individual might, in fact, be superior to the group in some way, but it is the attitude, not the superiority, that presents the obstruction. Sometimes blatant and other times carefully concealed, this attitude is often characteristic of a trustee representation style. Since superiority tends to discourage the free exchange of ideas, creativity, consensus building, and group esprit, it must be checked; this attitude can be preempted to a degree through a committee ground rule statement such as the one suggested in this chapter. (See the sample ground rule statement given previously.)

Stubbornness

Though stubbornness is an admirable quality when in the service of intellectual tenacity and strength of character, it can also reflect closed-mindedness—a decidedly unproductive quality in a committee member. Stubbornness can be characteristic of delegates or trustees, though it is a trait found in all kinds of people, and is not necessarily related to maturity level. Stubbornness often tends to be characteristic of the autonomous stage of development, when the driving force is a strong sense of independence. It is conformist-level behavior when motivated by a reluctance to deviate from the status quo, showing a predisposition to cling to that which is familiar and non-threatening. It is not usually characteristic of well-integrated, mature behavior. The chair or facilitator needs to look behind the attitude for the key to re-opening the communication channels that this attitude blocks.

Insensitivity

In this context, insensitivity does not refer to the rude, disrespectful, or careless treatment of others—though the inappropriateness of these behaviors should be understood. Insensitivity here refers to a participant's inability or unwillingness to empathize; to not feel and see an issue, idea, or proposal from another's perspective; to not feel another's pain and aspirations. Insensitivity refers to the inability or unwillingness to look at problems and solutions from the perspective of others; it blocks one's capacity to see potential win-win conflict resolutions. For delegates, sensitivity is a double-edged sword. While valuing responsiveness to the needs and aspirations of their constituencies, delegates cannot allow themselves to be persuaded by the needs or views of other constituencies; so insensitivity becomes a defense tactic. Trustees sometimes find themselves in a similar position. There are situations where their perceived responsibilities and the facts dictate one course of action; sensitivity to those affected by the decision dictates something quite different. In the end, the ability to empathize and act upon this empathy is a function of maturity—a higher stage of moral development. A delegate or trustee committee member functioning at a high level of development (the integrated stage) will be more likely to make a selfless, responsible decision. An individual functioning at the lower levels will tend to determine the decision based on his or her own perceived self-interest. Those in the middle will most likely follow their leaders.

GENERAL OBSTACLES TO CONSENSUS BUILDING

Besides the potentially obstructive behaviors of individuals such as those discussed above, there are other reasons why consensus building committees commonly fail.

Insufficient Meeting Time

Sometimes a committee does not stay together long enough, over a sufficiently concentrated period of time, to establish a sense of group identity. Or, if members do not work together long enough, they do not learn how to work with each other constructively.

External Time Pressure

This is a different problem than the one identified above. Sometimes a committee that has been working in earnest to come to consensus on some issue is informed that its decision is required immediately—or significantly ahead of schedule. In effect, the committee must try to reach consensus prematurely. When the committee tries to comply, there are two things that usually happen:

(1) The committee tries to reach closure on the issue with a vote. While usually perceived as fair and reasonable by the committee's members, the issue remains unresolved. Winners and losers are created by the short-circuited process.

(2) The decision itself is surrounded by unresolved cognitive dissonance, which occurs when two or more beliefs contradict each other. The consensus building process, left alone to run its course, would have resolved the conflict because an agreed-upon position somewhere within the span of the conflicting beliefs would have emerged as acceptable to the participants.

Unbalanced Representation

Sometimes the wrong people are on the committee. This is most likely to happen in the situation where different organizations or subgroups send representatives to some kind of central committee or task team. Sometimes one interest group has too many representatives on the committee. Sometimes a representative is at too low a level, organizationally, to usefully represent the leadership of the sending organization. If the representative is too high-level, other participants can feel intimidated or the representative feels as though a subordinate should have taken his or her place.

Insufficient Conflict or Controversy

That's right! It occurs when there is an inadequate diversity of opinion represented on the committee; if representative points of view on an issue are not present; if *groupthink* is at work; or if committee participants are too unwilling, feel too pressured, or are too insecure to disagree, debate, or confront one another over points of view or the interpretation of data. To achieve a meaningful consensus on a complex issue, there must first be cognitive dissonance, i.e., conflict. It is the constructive process of conflict that makes committee participants aware of an issue's inherent problems and implications. Conflict and controversy stimulate change, motivate problem-solving activity, and compel the group to focus, think through, and articulate a problem clearly and logically. Conflict and controversy ultimately enable self-understanding; they stimulate creativity; and when the conflict is finally resolved, give way to cohesiveness among members of the committee and those whom they represent.

Constructive use of conflict motivates committee members to seek solutions, seek more data, and exercise logic and reason. It is through controversy that members come to understand various perspectives. Controversy tends to encourage the forming of conclusions through thorough discussion. Also, the resolution of controversy builds relationships, and promotes reason, maturity, and social development. Conflict and controversy may be considered to have been constructive when an issue has been thoroughly considered and debated; understanding and relationships among participants have been strengthened; trust has been engendered; and, if the participants are reasonably happy with the resolution of the conflict, the committee is left in a position better able to resolve future issues. Constructive conflict is not only good, it is essential to the consensus building process. Managing conflict productively is the art of committee.

CHAPTER 4

Organization and Planning

IT WAS THE Roman philosopher Seneca who said something to the effect that *when one does not know which harbor he is heading for, no wind is right;* and so it is in practicing the art of committee. Without careful planning and a sense of what is to be accomplished, any committee or committee meeting is likely to wander and eventually flounder.

In this chapter, we will take a close, systematic look at how successful committee meetings are planned. We will also examine some ways to determine if a meeting went well, and if not, how to improve the next one.

WHY COMMITTEE MEETINGS FAIL

First, let's look at the main reasons why committee meetings often fail. Beyond obvious things like holding meetings in noisy uncomfortable places, or at inconvenient times or locations, common reasons for meeting failure usually revolve around one or more of the following:

(1) Poor or inadequate leadership

(2) Poor meeting management

(3) Poor time management

(4) Lack of organization

(5) Lack of participant responsibility

(6) Lack of clearly defined purpose

(7) Lack of closure or sense of progress

HOW COMMITTEES SUCCEED

For committees and committee meetings to be successful, both the chair and each participant must recognize that they have certain basic responsibilities to each other. These are as follows:

Responsibilities of the Chair

The chair or facilitator must define the committee's objective(s), and define the objective(s) for each meeting. He or she must develop an agenda and follow it unless the committee, as a whole, decides to alter it. The chair must try to start and end each meeting promptly; efficiently manage the time; limit and preside over discussion; elicit full participation; help resolve conflicts; clarify and summarize the conclusions or committee actions to be taken; delegate responsibilities; make effective use of subcommittees; and establish the time, place, and agenda for the next meeting. Most important, the chair or facilitator must follow through on the committee's work.

Following through includes distributing a memorandum to the committee participants on the major points that came out of the meeting—resolutions, conclusions, recommendations, future courses of action, etc.—and sending out the agenda and a review of responsibilities for the next meeting. If communication needs to extend beyond the committee to other individuals or organizations, this information should be disseminated as soon as possible after the meeting, and each committee member should receive copies or a summary of the substance of this communication. At some point the chair or facilitator should also provide a means for participants to evaluate the committee's meetings. The evaluation will provide a constructive channel for lingering participant frustration as well as useful feedback for the chair or facilitator on how meetings were perceived, how they were effective, and how they might be improved. The topic of meeting evaluation will be discussed later in this chapter.

Responsibilities of the Participants

Participants on successful committees must fulfill certain expectations. They must schedule meeting times and locations in their personal calendars; attend regularly; review the agenda; be prepared; and make sure they are clear on the committee's objectives and the objectives of each meeting. Participants should try to determine and define their roles on the committee (whom or what perspective they represent); listen, participate, and consider points of discussion with an open mind; follow the agenda; limit side conversations; and ask questions to clarify discussion points or discussion directions. Participants must also accept and conscientiously carry out committee assignments and tasks; review minutes or memorandums of understanding from the chair; take action as agreed; and provide candid and thoughtful evaluation to the chair on the committee's operation and meetings.

MEETING ORGANIZATION

To assist in meeting organization, many effective chairs use simple organizers such as the one provided in Figure 4.1. The major value of such a tool is that it forces the chairperson, and others planning meetings and committee work, to clarify their own thoughts and strategies before meeting with others.

Using the Meeting Plan Organizer

The Organizer, though a simple device, can be one of the successful committee chair's most useful tools. The section labeled *Committee Goals* should succinctly answer two broad questions:

(1) What are the key results to be accomplished by the committee?

(2) What must be achieved through the decision-making process?

Notice that these questions focus on both the substance of what is to be accomplished and the process through which the committee makes its decisions. Both concerns are of equal importance in practicing the art of committee.

The section on *Committee Participants* is a checking device for the chair; a means for reviewing committee representation with respect to such factors as organizational role, technical expertise or experience, and/or political constituency, etc. The participant makeup of a committee will determine the eventual quality and viability of the decisions and recommendations it makes. Therefore, the committee's membership should be carefully reviewed from the following perspectives:

(1) What expertise or experience does the committee need to accomplish its objectives?

(2) Whose commitment and support are necessary to carry out the committee's decisions or recommendations?

The participant list will also provide the chair with a reference for the organization of subcommittees and task assignments.

Next comes the task of developing specific meeting objectives. *Meet-*

Meeting Plan Organizer

Committee Goal(s):_____

_____

_____

Committee Participants
(and role, expertise, or
constituency) _____ _____

_____ _____

_____ _____

_____ _____

add additional lines as needed

Meeting Objective(s): _____

_____

_____

__Agenda /Timing: Item 1_____ Time_____mins

(tentative)   Item 2 _____ Time_____ "

Item 3 _____ Time _____ "

Item 4 _____ Time _____ "

add additional items as needed

Figure 4.1.

46

Committee Planner's Tool Kit: Organizer 2

Meeting Objectives Organizer

**Committee Goal: Develop Options and Determine the best
solution to problem X, by date Y.**
*Process Goal: Reach the decision through consensus
to ensure organizational commitment*

Achievement of Goal(s)

Objective 8   Select Options and recommend best solution

Objective 7   Deliberate over Options

Objective 6   Review and Discuss Options

Objective 5   Develop Options

Objective 4   Review and analyze data

Objective 3   Assign responsibilities for the identification & collection of data

Objective 2   Discuss goals; breakdown into tasks; establish work Plan.

Objective 1   Convene Committee: define and explain goal(s)

Figure 4.2.

ing Objectives represent the step-by-step plan a committee will follow
to achieve its substantive and process goals. Again, a simple organizer
will help in the development of these objectives (Figure 4.2). But each
committee usually requires its own, customized organizer depending on
the goals to be achieved. In developing an organizer, it is usually best to
work backwards from the committee goal(s), and ask, what steps are
necessary to systematically get to the goal? The organizer, developed in
this way, will help the chair to make sure that steps are not skipped; it
will also provide a basis for deciding the duration of the project and the
number of meetings that might be necessary to accomplish the committee's work.

Translating Meeting Objectives into Agenda Items

The last step in meeting planning is translating the meeting objectives into specific agenda items, with tentative item durations (Figure 4.3). For example, the chair might decide that there are about ninety minutes (a good meeting length, incidentally) available for the first meeting of the committee. The chair might then decide that a realistic expectation for that meeting would be to only accomplish objectives 1 and 2 from the meeting organizer (Figure 4.2).

Notice that tentative time estimates have been shown to the left of each agenda item in Figure 4.3 below. Whether or not to include these on the actual printed agenda is, to a large degree, a matter of personal style. Some leaders do not include time estimates because it gives the impression that the chair is too controlling. However, there are situations in which time estimates serve important functions. First, some committee members tend to use time as though it had no value. Time estimates on the agenda will help control these individuals. In other situations, time estimates serve to allow the chair to put everyone on notice that the committee is going to move forward briskly and deliberately, and that

Committee Planner's Tool Kit: Organizer 3

Agenda Organizer:

Objective 1   **Convene Committee: define and explain goal(s)**

Objective 2   Discuss goals; breakdown into tasks; establish work Plan.

The resulting Agenda items would then look something like this:

Meeting Agenda

10 min   1. **Introductions** *(introduce members and say what special thing each brings to the committee, or who each represents)*

15 min   2. **Explanation of Committee Goal(s)** *(The Chair defines the Committee's goals and clarifies through discussion)*

30 min   3. **Discussion of ComponentTasks** *(Committee breaks-down the goal into tasks)*

30 min   4.   **Begin Committee Work Plan and Sub-Committee Assignments**

5 min   5.   **Questions and Concerns** *(Chair provides opportunity for participants to ask questions on substance or process of the project so far.)*

6. **Adjourn** *(chair summarizes what has been accomplished at the meeting; establishes agenda for next meeting, and sets or confirms next meeting time, date, and location.)*

Figure 4.3.

the chair is highly organized. But whether or not time limits are suggested for the committee participants, the chair should estimate the length of each agenda item as a step in his or her own planning for meetings—if only to make certain that the expectations for each meeting can reasonably be met within the time available.

For subsequent meetings, the entire committee can help frame the agenda items and timings from the sequence of meeting objectives.

Physical Arrangements

Another important, yet often underappreciated, aspect of effective meeting planning is the task of providing the appropriate physical environment for the meeting itself. Though decidedly more mundane than the process of conceptualizing meeting objectives or organizing agendas, attending to the physical requirements of the committee is an important responsibility of the chair, and an important concern. As in any art form, the artist's technique is best observed in the details, and this is no less true in the art of committee.

Location

First, there is the location of the meeting. Routine meetings will probably be held on the premises in a regularly assigned room. But sometimes it makes sense to take the committee off-site to a retreat or conference center for concentrated, highly focused work. That is a decision that needs to be made.

Room Set-up

Then there is the meeting room itself. It should be appropriate to the size of the group. There should be room enough to seat committee members comfortably around a table—preferably a round or semicircular one, or on chairs in a circular or semicircular pattern in the room's center. Rooms that are too big tend to evaporate the group's energy, focus, and sense of intimacy. Rooms that are too small tend to be uncomfortable and warm. And unless highly ventilated, small rooms will sap the oxygen and energy from the meeting. However, there is room for some artistry in these choices. For example, when a committee needs to re-energize or convene dramatically for some important piece of information, crowding the committee into a room that is just a bit small, for a brief time, will create excitement and urgency. Rooms that are highly formal are appropriate only for formal meetings; but they can create a sense of formality when needed. Formal meeting rooms tend to inhibit members from relaxing. Formal meeting places, such as board rooms or hotel function rooms, are not appropriate for relaxed work sessions at which committee members need to create, brainstorm, analyze, discuss, exchange ideas, and interact informally with one another. Smaller, out of the way, informal, but neat and comfortable rooms are best for this purpose. To be certain that a room size is appropriate, set it up in advance, with the exact number of chairs, etc., needed by the group, and look at it.

Room temperature and ventilation are also important; a room temperature of approximately 68°F is generally considered optimal. A meeting room should be free from external noise and distractions. If possible the committee should be seated facing away from room entrances with backs to any outside windows. This will reduce distractions. Individuals should not be interrupted with messages, except in emergencies, since these interruptions also distract the meeting participants and interrupt group momentum. Holding the meeting off-site should all but eliminate these interruptions and keep participants fully focused.

There is the planning of the room set-up as well.

Seating Arrangements

Seating around a large round table is effective for committee meetings; psychologists advise that sitting in a circle tends to inhibit the focus of group energy onto any one individual. Seating around the more commonly encountered rectangular table focuses the group's energy alternately to either end of the table, the two traditional seating positions of power and command. An oval table tends to focus a participant's energy and attention onto the participant directly across the table. With the semicircular table, with participants all on one side, group energy is focused away from any single participant and onto a point in the center of the room—symbolically focusing the participants onto "the problem" as opposed to any particular participant. Therefore, that symbolic focal point is the optimal place for any group visual aid such as an easel, an overhead projector, a computer monitor or television screen, or a sub-committee presentation, etc.

A table tends to relax people. It provides a convenient work space, and, symbolically, a personal barrier. By removing that barrier and placing committee participants on chairs configured in a circular or semicircular pattern, the meeting becomes more open. Once acclimated to this set-up and relaxed with it, most participants will tend to respond more freely and more as individuals, though some might be made ill at ease and reserved. Removing the table tends to promote informality and break-down of formal organizational roles, and while some participants will be comfortable with this, others may not. The semicircle configuration, as at the table, will reduce some of this anxiety since energy is focused away from individuals and onto a central focal area. To make sure the committee congeals into a working unit, however, it is important that all participants stay seated in the circle or semicircle. In this particular set-up, anyone seated outside the circle is in the power or command position.

As indicated in Chapter 1, the committee seating arrangement can also be an important detail. It is best not to reinforce or enable cliques; if they are known about in advance, it is normally desirable to predistribute these individuals through an assigned seating arrangement, which will encourage all members to become better acquainted. If participants do not know one another or are only casually acquainted, preprinted nameplates or badges are appropriate.

Hospitality Arrangements

Hospitality arrangements need to be planned: coffee, fruit, and pastries, etc., tend to lower anxieties. Wine and cheese can be good for an introductory icebreaker or final wrap-up meeting. These refreshments can change the tone of the meeting dramatically.

The Meeting Plan Checklist

Figure 4.4 provides another useful organizational device—a meeting plan check list. This will allow the chair or an assistant to make certain that the various planning details involved in establishing a meeting have been carried out.

Meeting Plan Check List

Physical Requirements

___   *Meeting location selected*

___   *Meeting room selected and reserved*

___   *Meeting room set-up appropriately (chairs/table etc)*

___   *Seating determined (if necessary)*

___   *Name tags or name plates for participants prepared*

___   *Hospitality arrangements made*

___   *Other details (parking vouchers, lunch menu etc)*

Planning Requirements

___   *Committee objective(s) established*

___   *Participants selected and confirmed for meeting*

___   *Meeting objectives established*

___   *Meeting agenda prepared and multi-copied*

___   *Meeting materials organized, multi-copied and collated*

___   *Meeting type/style defined (problem solving, executive, creative-brainstorming etc)*

___   *Meeting leadership type determined (authority figure as chair or independent facilitator)*

Figure 4.4.

Meeting Operation

___   *Explain committee and meeting objectives*

___   *Establish or review ground rules*

___   *Seek to achieve maximum participation*

___   *Keep meeting on agenda*

___   *Encourage conflict of ideas (cognitive dissonance)*

___   *Maintain meeting control*

___   *Maintain meeting time frame and momentum*

___   *Assign specific responsibilities for tasks*

Adjournment

___   *Summarize meeting*

___   *Establish next meeting (time and place)*

___   *Establish agenda for next meeting*

___   *Review and record meeting's major points, outcomes and specific charges to individuals or subcommittees*

Evaluate Meeting

Figure 4.4. (continued).

MEETING EVALUATION

In her own helpful manual on meetings entitled, *Effective Meeting Skills,* author Marion E. Hayes advises: "Effective meetings occur when leaders and participants work to find a better way to get the job done. Participants come to a meeting with ideas, skills, knowledge, and experience. The leader's job is to create an environment where evaluation becomes a normal part of the process."[7]

There are really three basic ways to evaluate a meeting.

(1) Self-evaluation by the leader: In this method the chair or facilitator takes a brief time after the meeting he or she has just led, and reflects on how the meeting went. What worked well? Was the agenda accomplished? Was participation fluid and open? What kind of meeting was it supposed to be? Was the leadership style appropriate and effective? Was the meeting well-managed and controlled? Were all the physical arrangements appropriate? What could have been done better?

(2) Evaluation by a trained observer: In this method, an individual who understands what makes meetings effective, observes objectively from the back of the room; takes notes on the process of how the meeting was conducted and how problems were handled effectively, how problems were unaddressed, and how they might have been anticipated, avoided, or handled better. The observer also makes notes on the leadership style being exhibited, and on how time was effectively or ineffectively managed. After the meeting, the observer meets with the chair or facilitator; shares the observations, and makes recommendations for improvement.

(3) Evaluation by the participants: Participants themselves can provide highly useful responses. And the process of monitoring this information can be an informal one. The meeting leader simply pays close attention to participant behavior, body language, facial expressions, and reactions as the meeting progresses. For some meetings it might be worth asking participants to complete an evaluation form, its purpose being to make future meetings more efficient and productive. The form could be a rating system upon which participants grade various aspects of the meeting (e.g., organization, beginning

---

[7]Hayes, Marion E. *Effective Meeting Skills.* Los Altos, CA: Crisp Publications, Inc., 1988, p. 64.

and ending on time, opportunities to speak, clarity of objectives, progress toward task, level of constructive controversy, leadership style, adequacy of "process" to arrive at consensus, etc.). However, participants generally tend to be in a hurry to leave after a meeting has concluded, in which case the chair or facilitator might not get evaluation results that are very carefully considered or thought out. Follow-up meetings or telephone conversations with individual committee participants can provide a means for the chair to get opinions, but private conversation with selected participants can give other participants the impression that there is an "in" group on the committee. All things considered, it is probably best to build places into the meeting agendas themselves, at strategic points, for participants to complete a meeting evaluation form. The results of the evaluation can be shared at the next meeting, and ways for improving the meetings can be discussed by the committee, or simply commented upon by the chair, as future guidelines or as "the committee's suggestions for improving meetings." Remember, all people like to have their suggestions taken seriously.

A refinement on this idea is to prepare separate meeting evaluation forms—each concentrating on some specific aspect of meeting management. Pass one out at one meeting, pass out a different one at the next, etc., or, if the committee is a large one, different members could get different evaluation forms—each focusing on a different aspect of the meeting(s).

Meeting Evaluation Forms

Figures 4.5–4.9 are sample meeting evaluation forms. Three of them focus primarily on one aspect of meeting organization or management (e.g., committee objectives, agendas, and process). Two of these forms are more general in scope, and would come later.

Evaluations provide important feedback on how meetings are perceived and how they need to be improved. While all participants share, to some degree, the responsibility for making the most of each committee meeting, the major responsibility for seeking this input and acting upon it to make needed improvements is, in the end, a leadership task—and just one of the many such tasks we shall see in the next chapter. Chapter 5 focuses on the nature of leadership and the critical role leadership, itself, plays in the art of committee.

Committee Purpose (Objectives)

1. To what extent do you understand the objectives of this committee?

      1   2   3   4   5
not at   completely
all

2. To what extent do you think others on the committee understand the Objectives?

      1   2   3   4   5
not at   completely
all

3. To what extent did the meeting make progress toward achievement of the objectives?

      1   2   3   4   5
not at   to great
all   extent

4. To what extent was the meeting well organized ?

      1   2   3   4   5
not at   to great
all   extent

5. To what extent did the meeting agenda lead toward accomplishment of the committee's objectives ?

      1   2   3   4   5
not at   to great
all   extent

6. To what extent does the committee stay on task?

      1   2   3   4   5
not at all   completely

Figure 4.5. *Meeting Evaluation Form #1 (adapted from Hayes, Marion E. 1988.* Effective Meeting Skills. *Los Altos, CA: Crisp Publications, Inc.).*

Agendas

1. To what extent are meeting agendas circulated in advance?
   1   2   3   4   5
   never   always

2. To what extent are the agendas followed in meetings?

   1   2   3   4   5
   never   always

3. To what extent do meetings start and end on time?

   1   2   3   4   5
   never   always

4. To what extent are agenda items accomplished within the time
   frames of the committee's meetings?

   1   2   3   4   5
   never   always

5. To what extent are committee members consulted in planning
   agendas for future meetings?

   1   2   3   4   5
   never   always

6. To what extent do agendas for each meeting guide the committee
   toward accomplishment of the committee's objectives?

   1   2   3   4   5
   never   always

Figure 4.6. Meeting Evaluation Form #2 (adapted from Hayes, Marion E. 1988.
Effective Meeting Skills. *Los Altos, CA: Crisp Publications, Inc.).*

57

Process

1. To what extent are differences of opinion among committee members encouraged and explored?

$$1 \quad 2 \quad 3 \quad 4 \quad 5$$
not at all   always

2. To what extent do committee members show respect for each other's points of view ?

$$1 \quad 2 \quad 3 \quad 4 \quad 5$$
not at all   always

3. To what extent do all committee members participate in Discussions?

$$1 \quad 2 \quad 3 \quad 4 \quad 5$$
not at all   always

4. To what extent do committee members work constructively with each other ?

$$1 \quad 2 \quad 3 \quad 4 \quad 5$$
not at all   always

5. To what extent are responsibilities for committee assignments delegated to committee members ?

$$1 \quad 2 \quad 3 \quad 4 \quad 5$$
not at all   a great deal

6. To what extent is discussion adequate before decisions are reached?

$$1 \quad 2 \quad 3 \quad 4 \quad 5$$
not enough   too much
discussion   discussion

Figure 4.7. *Meeting Evaluation Form #3 (adapted from Hayes, Marion E. 1988.* Effective Meeting Skills. *Los Altos, CA: Crisp Publications, Inc.).*

General

1. To what extent did the meeting achieve its stated objectives?

$$1 \quad 2 \quad 3 \quad 4 \quad 5$$
not at all   completely

2. To what extent did you feel you were able to represent your particular interest(s)?

$$1 \quad 2 \quad 3 \quad 4 \quad 5$$
not at all   completely

3. To what extent were you asked to provide ideas?

$$1 \quad 2 \quad 3 \quad 4 \quad 5$$
not at all   completely

4. When committee decisions are made, to what extent are the action steps "followed through " by committee members and/or the Chair?

$$1 \quad 2 \quad 3 \quad 4 \quad 5$$
not at all   completely

5. Which portion of this meeting did you find most useful?

_____

_____

6. Which aspects of this meeting were least helpful to you?

_____

_____

7. How could this meeting have been more productive?

_____

_____

Figure 4.8. *Meeting Evaluation Form #4 (adapted from Hayes, Marion E. 1988.* Effective Meeting Skills. *Los Altos, CA: Crisp Publications, Inc.).*

	General			1= Never 2=Infrequently 3=Sometimes 4=Frequently 5=Always	
Suggest the **extent** to which:	1	2	3	4	5
1. Participants had opportunities to express opinions	—	—	—	—	—
2. Different points of view were encouraged	—	—	—	—	—
3. Participants listened to each other's ideas.	—	—	—	—	—
4. Individual members dominated the meetings	—	—	—	—	—
5. Participants seemed annoyed with each other	—	—	—	—	—
6. Some participant's ideas were ignored	—	—	—	—	—
7. Participants seemed confused about committee objectives	—	—	—	—	—
8. Participants seemed confused about meeting objectives	—	—	—	—	—
9. Sub-committees were used effectively	—	—	—	—	—
10. Participants support the committee's decisions; consensus is achieved.	—	—	—	—	—

Figure 4.9. *Meeting Evaluation Form #5 (adapted from Hayes, Marion E. 1988.* Effective Meeting Skills. *Los Altos, CA: Crisp Publications, Inc.).*

CHAPTER 5

Leadership and How to Develop It

FINALLY WE COME to the single most critical factor in whether committees do or do not succeed in their missions, *leadership*. It would be ingenuous to attempt to define the precise qualities of intellect and style that must come together to make an effective leader. It is conventional wisdom that leaders, in general, are born; or that they develop qualities that are unique among other men and women. These qualities are largely intuitive, but forged through the interaction of personality, environment, experience, ambition, and opportunity. However, we also know that effective committee leaders can be trained and cultivated. One can learn the principles, observe good models, and practice the skills. Add measures of intuition, perceptiveness, intelligence, and, with luck, a pinch of aptitude, and an extremely effective committee leader can be created.

LEADERS EMERGE

Yet in reality, skilled committee leaders are often neither born nor created. They simply find themselves in the situation. An individual becomes a committee chair by three primary routes: election, succession, or appointment. In the public and volunteer sectors, individuals are usually elected to important committees (e.g., finance committees, boards of education, boards of selectmen, church boards, community councils, and the boards of various service organizations, etc.). These "committees," in turn, often elect their own officers, including a chair. In such instances the elected chair may or may not really have the skills to lead what amounts to a committee—so hopefully this book will be of some help. A similar situation exists when an individual "succeeds" (if only temporarily) to the chair from the vice chair, or from another role on the committee. Again, this is the circumstance of finding oneself in the role of leading a committee, perhaps without adequate training or experience.

There are, however, instances in business as well as government and education, where individuals are appointed, or simply invited, to participate on important committees by some authority. In these situations, the appointed committee might have, as part of its charge, the responsibility to elect its own chair or leader. But more commonly, the chair is either an officer of the authority itself, or an individual appointed by the authority before the selection of the other committee members. Here, presumably, the chair does have the necessary skills to lead, and is usually given a significant leg-up on success, even before the committee is convened—the opportunity to shape the task as well as the membership of the committee with whom he or she will work. While there are situations where the following applies to elected chairpersons as well, the appointed chair has the opportunity to conceptualize his or her task in advance—and participate in structuring it.

THE LEADERSHIP ROLE: PHASE 1

Conceptualizing the Task

The first step for a prospective committee leader (ideally, before accepting leadership responsibility) is to size up the situation—to understand the task. And beyond just understanding both the letter and spirit of what will be the committee's charge, it is the responsibility of the committee leader, the appointing authority, or both, to decide:

(1) Whether a committee is really needed, and if so,

(2) What kind of a committee is needed? (an executive committee, creative/brainstorming committee, or a problem-solving committee that must develop consensus decisions or positions on a problem, issue, or task).

Determining What Kind of Committee Is Needed

Understanding what kind of committee is most appropriate to the task is the first basic, a priori decision in committee management. Organizing a committee to cause consensus on a task that really requires a brainstorming group of participants to create new ideas is a fundamental strategic error. Organizing a committee of creative brainstormers on technical issues to provide technical information to a CEO who simply wants to collect the best possible technical opinions to help him or her make an executive decision is probably a waste of everyone's time.

Asking and Answering the Fundamental Questions

The fundamental questions to be asked and answered before any committee is formed and charged are:

- What is the task to be accomplished?
- What is the nature of the task?
- What kind of committee is needed?
- When must the task be completed?
- Is the task one that can be effectively addressed by a committee?
- What is the committee's authority?
- What are the committee's resources?

The Committee Charge

The next consideration is the committee's charge, the statement of what the committee is expected to do—the goal to be achieved. Both creative and problem-solving committees start their work with a charge. A good charge is specific about what the general goal of the committee's work is to be, particularly in terms of what the committee's products are to be. Is the committee to produce options and recommendations, or is it to produce final decisions? What is the committee's authority? To whom or to what body does it report? In what form(s) are its products to be delivered—a written report, a public presentation, or both? All these elements should be in the charge, along with an indication of when the committee's work is to be completed, and to whom the committee's work is to be delivered. Ideally, a good charge is not more specific than it has to be, leaving the final shaping of the work to the committee itself. For example, a charge saying that a committee is to *develop, analyze, and evaluate optional responses* to a given circumstance, problem, or event and to *produce a written report and presentation of the committee's evaluation of each option, with a recommended course of action, to the Chief Executive Officer by such and such a date,* is a charge that is both conceptual enough for the committee to help shape, and specific enough that the committee should understand what is expected.

However, sometimes it is necessary to provide more direction to a committee through a more specific charge. In this situation, the charge is focused at a lower level of detail, providing the committee with the component tasks inherent in achieving the broader conceptual goal, already broken-down and specified. It would then remain for the committee to address the specific tasks, do its analysis, and present its written report—perhaps with a recommendation for action, though not necessarily.

It is the chair's task to understand not only the relevance of each task but the nature and importance of the goal itself—what is behind the charge. Again, there are some critical questions to be asked and answered before proceeding.

Understanding the Charge

- Are the tasks stated clearly?
- Can the tasks be completed in the time requested and with the human and physical resources available?
- What will be the committee's authority?
- To whom will the committee report its decisions or recommendations?

There is an important caveat here. Many a committee, and committee chair, have found themselves in trouble by not clearly understanding their charge. A wise prospective committee chair will view the charge as a contract, the details and expectations of which are best made clear right at the beginning. Once the parties have complete agreement on what the committee is expected to do, then the "chair designate" can confidently accept the responsibility and begin helping to organize his or her committee.

The ABCs of Committee Formation

To the degree that the chair can choose or influence the selection of the committee's eventual membership, he or she should take full advantage of the opportunity. But no matter who is doing the committee selection, the following guidelines are advised.

Breadth of Experience and Knowledge

Seek to bring the widest possible range of viewpoints, relevant skills, and experience to the committee. It is through this diversity and richness that the committee will eventually draw its strength and power.

Diversity of Viewpoint

Where representation in the decision-making process is an important consideration, or where representation from various constituencies is necessary to insure smooth implementation and good communication of committee decisions, seek the representatives who are relatively extreme or outspoken in their viewpoints. This concept I refer to as the "All the tigers in the cage principle." If the committee's decisions or recommendations are likely to be controversial and/or must be presented, sold, or defended to other groups later, it is best to have potential predators on the committee—involved in the process. Arguably, this does make the committee much more difficult to lead, and could even derail the committee's work in the early stages, but what is gained from having the toughest critics at the table can pay off big in successful implementation at the end of the line.

The Requisite Competencies

While including those on the committee who, for one reason or other, must be included, pay careful attention to the special skills, knowledge, experience, or competencies each prospective committee member can contribute to the task. Certainly, there are individuals on committees who are included principally because of their organizational role or because they represent some constituency. However, there may also have to be people added who have more highly developed skills, relevant experience, and/or expertise to help the committee in competently addressing its task. Though this may seem obvious, think of the boards and advisory committees that are made up of prominent citizens and highly successful people from impressive but unrelated fields. How often are these committees asked to make recommendations on matters well outside their participants' areas of direct experience, and how often do the resulting recommendations betray a dilettante perspective, and end up irrelevant at best. This can be easily avoided by including a few additional participants with relevant experience and "knowledge" on the committee.

THE LEADERSHIP ROLE: PHASE 2

The role of the leader of almost any kind of committee is to summon forth, harness, and apply the knowledge, creativity, experience, abilities, talents, and resources of all those participating in the task. It is the leader who manages the deliberation process to bring about decisions that are credible and practicable. Either personally or through others, the leader must define, shape and produce the committee's product(s), and manage the processes through which the committee operates. Not surprisingly then, it can be postulated that it is principally through the leadership role(s) that one practices the art of committee.

Leadership and the Chair

To Lead or Not to Lead

Note that, in the above paragraph, the word *leader* was used instead of chair because these roles are not always one and the same; there is an important distinction. The chair is the individual charged with the responsibility of the committee and its work. He or she may or may not be the person actually leading the committee meetings. The leader could be either the chair or a facilitator. The leader is the individual empowered to manage the proceedings—lead the committee's meetings. Therefore, one of the first tasks the chair must decide is whether to:

(1) Lead the committee process him or herself
(2) Make use of a facilitator
(3) Lead the meeting him or herself in the style of a facilitator

This is an important strategic decision by the chair, as it defines what his/her role in the deliberation process must be. If the chair is also a hierarchical leader representing the "management" or administration of the organization, the choice to use an independent facilitator to actually run the meetings could be a wise decision. For one, the chair, when functioning as the committee leader, must remain as neutral as possible; otherwise, the deliberation process does not unfold from within the committee. As the leader of any kind of committee (other than the executive committee where the chair is simply looking for ideas and assistance in making decisions) the chair's primary job is to "manage," not ramrod, the process. To do this, the chair must submerge his or her own point of view, which means that the "management" point of view might not be adequately represented in the deliberation process. By using an independent facilitator, the chair may assume an active role as a participant on the committee.

The Chair as Leader

As indicated above, the chair has some options when it comes to the role he or she assumes on a committee. On committees where consensus is to be achieved, the chair may wish to be an active participant, functioning as any other member of the committee. Or, the chair might wish to take on the role of meeting leader or facilitator; in which case, the chair must strive to remain neutral, and simply manage the process, not engage in putting forth or defending a point of view or "position" on a given issue.

Responsibilities of the Chair

Whether or not the chair decides to lead, it is still his or her responsibility to focus the committee—to explain the charge; explain what it is that the committee has been convened to accomplish; and initiate the process of focusing the committee on its assignment.

Focusing is best accomplished through discussion. It is the chair's role to initiate this discussion by presenting the charge within the context of its broader organizational or philosophical importance; to place the assignment of the committee into appropriate perspective against the organization's past, future, or larger strategic goals; to express the importance and implications of the committee's assignment as to how it will fit into the "big picture," and then to encourage questioning and free discussion of the specifics of the charge, including key words—their meanings, values, and implications. This is called focusing the committee, and its purpose is to establish a thorough understanding, among committee members, of not only what the committee has been convened to accomplish, but why the work is important.

It is the chair's responsibility to "pull the committee together," and to give the committee's mission a positive, forward thrust. This is accomplished not only by focusing the committee, through open discussion, on what is to be accomplished and why, but by introducing the committee's members to each other, in terms of the special roles, experiences, skills and resources, etc., each brings to the task. It is also accomplished by setting forth the tentative timeline for the committee's work: *when* the committee's mission is to be completed; any *targets* that have been (even tentatively) established; exactly *what kinds of products* are expected at the end of the process; and *to whom* the products are to be presented (the audience).

(1) Typical committee products
  • decision(s)
  • recommendation(s)
  • options
(2) Typical forms of presentation
  • written report(s)
  • oral presentation(s)

The chair's judgment and persistence in not moving forward until the committee has thoroughly discussed the charge, is the first step in practicing the art of committee.

The Facilitator as Leader

When the chair decides not to lead the meetings, a facilitator performs this function, and the leadership role shifts from chair to facilitator.

The Facilitator's Role

The meeting facilitator, you will recall, was characterized earlier (in Chapter 3) as "the meeting chauffeur." The facilitator is not usually an organizational authority figure, and is, therefore, not normally the individual in the best position to "set the destination" and focus (as described above). This is why the chair best performs that organizational task. The facilitator picks up the leadership role after the committee focusing step. The meeting facilitator runs the meetings and guides the committee through the process of achieving its work program, but is otherwise not a participant in the decision-making arena. In some situations, an experienced chair might have the ability to move in and out of both roles, depending on the topic and nature of the committee's undertaking. This, however, requires a highly skilled and experienced chair, who enjoys a high degree of credibility and trust from the members of his or her committee.

Establishing Meeting Tone and Style

Once the committee has been properly charged and focused, and it has been established whether a chair or a facilitator will fulfill the meeting leadership function, it is the leader's task to establish the committee's operational tone and style. This is essentially a statement of attitude, and it begins with reading the committee's ground rules. A simple, sample ground rules statement was provided earlier on page 36. In essence, the ground rules statement should show an intent: that the committee will tap, rather than stifle, the contributions, motivations, resources, experiences, perceptions, and viewpoints of all its participants, and that the committee will value the attitudes, opinions, and relationships of the committee's members as resources to be applied to accomplishing the committee's primary goal of completing its responsibilities as set forth in the charge.

The next step is to advise committee members that they will be involved in the planning and structuring of future meetings and the development of the committee's work plan. The work plan is the statement of tasks to be carried out by the committee, subcommittees, and individual members in accomplishing the committee's charge. While this affirmation of committee participation in decision making may not be necessary when the "style" of the chair or facilitator is well-known by the participants, it does help to establish a collegial tone as the committee embarks on its work.

Centering the Task(s)

Whether the committee leadership function is turned over to a facilitator or whether leadership remains with the chair, the next job is to begin breaking down the charge into tasks and a work plan, through a process called centering. In preparation for this stage, it is important that the leader (chair or facilitator) has done his or her homework, and anticipated, if only tentatively, the tasks involved in addressing the charge—as illustrated and discussed in Chapter 4. Centering is discussing the general charge and each of the component tasks in all their ramifications, defining relevant or ambiguous terms and word meanings, and establishing standards as to what "accomplishment" means to different committee members and, ultimately, to the committee as a whole. This centering process should involve all members of the committee in examining, disassembling, re-defining, reconstructing, and shaping specific tasks, breaking them into subtasks to be centered themselves. Centering can be a long, frustrating process or a very short exercise, depending on the complexity and the ramifications of the tasks. However, the centering process, executed patiently and properly, should develop a sharper, deeper understanding of the committee's charge and each task, along with an understanding of the standards by which the

Table 5.1. The Tasks of Leadership.

- The leader must take responsibility for planning.
  - Develop a preliminary work plan for the committee's review and further development (see Chapter 4).
  - Create the agendas and take on committee communication and follow-through responsibilities.
  - Supervise, or oversee, all meeting arrangements (place, room set-up, refreshments).

- The leader manages the meetings.
  - Remains neutral in committee deliberations.
  - Draws out and involves each member of the committee.
  - Anticipates the various functions that must be performed by committee members and makes judgments about which individuals can best perform these functions.
  - Stimulates and maintains meeting momentum; keeps the meeting moving forward.
  - Mediates opposing views; restates or summarizes participant positions for clarity.
  - Maintains order and decorum: meeting style and tone centered around mutual respect.
  - Establishes environment that allows the meetings to run from within: encourages active discussion, the expression of opposing viewpoints, debate, teamwork, experimentation.
  - Creates communication channels for ideas and information from each member of the committee.
  - Establishes and organizes subcommittees with clear directions and responsibilities.
  - Assigns individual responsibilities for committee tasks.
  - Takes responsibility for seeing that committee notes or minutes are maintained and regularly shared on a timely basis.
  - Periodically creates mental pictures for the committee, depicting issues of agreement and disagreement.
  - Periodically creates mental picture for committee of where they are in terms of the work program and charge.
  - Apprises the committee participants of where they are in the process: how the work is progressing; what has been accomplished; what remains to be done.
  - Leads the committee to consensus.

- The chair produces committee products.
  - Takes responsibility for the creation, production, and presentation of the committee's recommendations, options, decisions, and written reports.
  - Organizes the committee's oral presentations.

70

committee's work will be judged. The ability to center each task is an essential leadership tool in the art of committee.

Whether it is the committee's chair or a facilitator who assumes the leadership role, there are a number of essential tasks that the leader must successfully carry out in effectively practicing the art of committee (Table 5.1).

MANAGING PEOPLE AND IDEAS

The art of committee, then, is fundamentally the art of managing the interaction of people and ideas. And to guide this process, there are some key principles for the chair, or a facilitator, as leader, to establish and maintain.

Eight Principles of Effective Committee Interaction

(1) Each committee member should come to meetings prepared to participate, both in terms of background information, assignments, and attitude.

(2) Committee members must be encouraged, and if necessary led, to express their views clearly and logically and to follow up with illustrations and examples for clarification; then to listen to others' reactions and views before pressing their point further.

(3) All participants must be encouraged to express agreement or disagreement with another's views. It is no service to the committee for participants to agree with or leave unchallenged another's view, just to be polite or to maintain a friendly atmosphere in the meeting. When one participant offers an idea or point of view, it is the committee's responsibility to react and give feedback.

(4) It is the responsibility of each participant as well as the leader, to make certain all understand what a participant is saying. To this end, it is often the role of the leader to restate, clarify through questions, and/or lead discussion around participants' views to be certain they are examined and clearly understood by all.

(5) All participants' views and opinions must be respected.

(6) Participants must take ownership of their ideas, attitudes, feelings and points of view. Phrases like "some people think," used for other than actually reporting on what others are perceived to believe, tend to negate the ownership of ideas, attitudes, and perceptions.

(7) Participants must practice careful listening. The chair must provide opportunities for participants to paraphrase, accurately and non-judgmentally, what another has said. Careful listening also means being able to read and articulate the attitudes and/or feelings behind what is said.

(8) The leader, as well as the other participants, must also listen perceptively, noting consistencies or inconsistencies between a participant's past and present statements or positions.

Negative Practices

Beyond these principles, the chair (or facilitator), as committee leader, has a special responsibility to be on the lookout for certain negative practices that impede effective communication. Below are the major and most common impediments.

Unclear or Ambiguous Language

Use of unclear or ambiguous language: When a committee participant speaks, his or her language must be clear and unambiguous. If the chair or facilitator senses it is not, he or she must ask for clarification or elaboration before moving on. Each participant must say what he or she means—clearly. But to help, the leader may need to restate or elaborate on another's statements to be certain they are clearly understood by all.

Mixed messages: Conflicting and/or inconsistent statements by the same speaker produce a mixed message. It is the job of the leader to remind the speaker of these conflicting statements, and to tactfully help, or even require, the speaker to resolve them, as they occur, so the committee is always clear about what the speaker thinks and what his or her view really is.

Statements That Conflict with Body Language

Mixed messages are also sent: when statements conflict with facial expressions or body language. Today, the notion of body language is well-established and generally perceived in our culture—so much so that it can be manipulated by participants on a committee. Yet, there are some examples of body language that tend to be more unconscious. The perceptive committee leader or participant should be alert to cues such as those listed in Table 5.2.

Table 5.2. Body Language Cues.

- A rigid body tends to associate with unbending, rigid ideas or attitudes.
- A raised chin tends to associate with a courageous, optimistic view.
- A thrust jaw often indicates anger or determination.
- A slumping body often suggests a lazy, sloppy or defeated personality.
- Raised shoulders and pulled-in neck suggest fear.
- The eyes can carry anger, fear, amusement, agreement, directness, evasiveness, duplicity, and more.
- Lines on the forehead can show surprise or uncertainty.
- The voice can indicate strain, timidity, agitation, aggressiveness, reluctance, hesitation, thoughtfulness, carefulness, cautiousness, or enthusiasm.

Over-generalization

Over-generalization: Broad summarizing statements, observations, and opinions by committee participants have a way of precluding discussion and obscuring logic. The generalizations may or may not be true, but the committee will never know unless these statements are questioned, examined, defended, or otherwise dealt with.

Transferring onto Others

Transferring one's own thoughts or motives to another: As discussed earlier, each individual comes to the committee with his or her own baggage. One participant should not try to ascribe motives or assume ways of thinking to another that are not somehow supported by observation and/or reason.

Posturing

Self image is important to everyone, but it cannot be allowed to become an impediment to constructive meeting participation. Individuals who are overly concerned about the quality, thoughtfulness, and articulateness of their own statements, and those of others, cannot participate freely and spontaneously in the give-and-take of committee meetings. It is for this reason that pubic meetings—particularly those covered by the press—are very often meetings in name only; they are more often quasi-theatrical events; the real meeting happens somewhere else or simply doesn't occur at all. For a real committee meeting to be effective, each participant must feel secure that every statement he or anyone else makes does not have to be brilliant, persuasive, or set forth a particular position. Candor and openness must be present at committee meetings to achieve a healthy give-and-take of ideas, beliefs, information, and points of view.

Vetoing

There is another form of meeting obstruction that must be avoided by the chair or facilitator—vetoing. Where consensus is to be achieved in a committee, prematurely cutting off discussion on an issue, using the

Table 5.3. What the Leader Can Do to Positively Resolve Conflicts between or among Committee Members.

(1) Identify the areas of common ground between members in conflict. When these areas are pointed out, the members in conflict have an opportunity to back off gracefully. The areas of common ground can also be the basis for consensus building later on.

(2) Dilute personality clashes by inviting participation from other members of the committee; ask for other ideas and feedback on the issue in dispute.

(3) Broaden the discussion. In this maneuver, the leader notes that it seems a bit too early for conclusions. The leader then suggests that the committee review the issue under discussion from a number of different perspectives. This can refocus those individuals who are already set in their point of view. It also saves the direct conflict for a later time when emotions are better under control so more reasoned conclusions can prevail, or a consensus can be achieved.

(4) Seek more information. Here, the leader asks for additional information or appoints a subcommittee to collect more facts on the issue under dispute—even if the dispute appears to be more an interpersonal problem between members. The task of collecting additional information, in itself, tends to defuse over-emotional conflict.

(5) When all else fails, briefly adjourn the meeting (to refresh coffee cups, etc.). When the meeting is reconvened, after the break, introduce a new topic (from the agenda) for committee discussion.

power of the leadership role to unilaterally remove an issue from consideration, flatly refusing to place an issue on a committee's agenda, or sacrificing the neutrality and objectivity of the leadership role to support a minority or non-consensus position, are all behaviors that destroy constructive group process and committee morale.

Techniques of Meeting Management

The art of committee encompasses the use of a repertoire of meeting management techniques, since these are used to help the leader in the task of managing the interaction of people and ideas.

Table 5.3 contains five useful strategies for managing confrontations when they occur between committee members.

MANAGING PARTICIPANT BEHAVIOR

There are techniques for dealing effectively and sensitively with the behavior problems of individual participants. Here are a few useful ones.

The Cardinal Rules

Maintain Eye Contact

The first cardinal rule for effectively using any conflict or behavior management technique is never lose direct eye contact with the subject. With direct, non-blinking eye contact, almost any technique will be effective; without it, the leader is not exerting dynamic, personal control over the situation.

Treat All with Respect

Always treat people with respect, even when some individuals are rude and "out-of-line." The leader can maintain control by never entering the dialogue emotionally; by speaking quietly and slowly but firmly; and by treating even outrageous remarks with a polite response that acknowledges the speaker's frustration. However, there is a thin line here. The leader has a responsibility to protect individual committee members from attack, and it might be necessary to quietly but firmly tell a strident speaker that his or her remarks or behavior are not appropriate; that every participant deserves to be treated with civility and respect. The leader should then quickly return to the principal discussion, address another speaker, and draw others into the conversation, allowing emotions to cool while continuing to move the meeting forward with other participants.

Avoid Personalizing

Never make a confrontation personal; the leader must always stay emotionally detached and task oriented when addressing participants and participant behaviors. Sometimes an individual committee participant persistently exhibits a negative attitude.

Head shaking, muttering, overt nay-saying, or making fun of others' ideas and comments are all manifestations of a negative attitude. To some degree, this has been addressed earlier (see our discussion of "deserters" and "dissenters" in Chapter 2). Recall that we advised, first, that if the behavior persists, it is usually best that the chair confront the individual privately and ask what all the negativism is about. Remember, certain negative gestures like squirming, eye rolling, etc., are often reflexes; it is possible that pointing out the behavior to the individual in a polite, constructive way might be enough to curb it. But if necessary, another effective way to address negative behavior is to force it into the open; in effect, to require the participant to justify himself. For example, the chair (or facilitator) might politely interrupt the proceedings and say: "so and so, I don't think you are buying this line of reasoning. Tell us what your concerns are—precisely." It is the "precisely" word that is operative in this technique. Drawing out the nay-sayer and requiring that participant to explain, in detail, the basis for his or her negative response or attitude toward a certain idea or suggestion, in effect, turns the tables on the nay-sayer. It puts him or her on the defensive, and puts that person's views, or the fact that he or she can't articulate them, up for comment and evaluation by others. The technique can be particularly effective if the leader is skilled enough to drag this inquiry out—just to the point that the individual in the spotlight and/or other committee members begin to feel slightly uncomfortable. *But never personalize.* The leader, to effectively use this technique, must stay personally detached and focused on the nay-sayer's words and attitude only as they relate to the subject at hand.

Other Aspects of Behavior Management

Beyond conflict management, there is also the less stressful aspect of what I call *annoyance management*—what to do with whisperers and interrupters, for example.

Whisperers are the easiest with which to deal, and the direct approach has always worked best for me. Simply call on one of them "so everyone can hear what you have got to contribute." Sometimes this has to be done a couple of times, but usually people get the point. In more persistent cases, the leader should come up with some pretext for rearranging the seating, and simply separate the whisperers, permanently. Interrupters might be overly enthusiastic or just plain rude participants. The leader can deal with this best by holding up his or her hand, in a gesture that says wait your turn.

A variation on this behavior is the individual who interrupts to interpret what another is trying to say. Here, again, the solution is usually simple; the leader should look at the person trying to speak and ask if the interrupter has represented his views accurately; then point out to the interrupter that the process will actually go faster if everyone is allowed to speak for themselves.

There are other kinds of annoyances, of course, but the principle being put forth here is to deal with them quickly and directly. Do not let annoyances persist meeting after meeting. Deal with them early and deal with them decisively. It is best for the leader to let everyone on the committee know, by his or her polite but firm corrective style, which behaviors are tolerated and which ones are not.

Group Techniques

It is important to note that sometimes committees do not operate as envisioned; they stall or somehow develop difficulties. Here are a few techniques to help the committee get back on track.

Transaction Analysis

Transaction analysis can be useful. This technique focuses participants on how the members of the committee actually interact with each other and how the committee operates. Someone, often an outside observer, carefully watches a meeting and notes who does what; how participants respond to each other; where the committee goes off track; whether or not it is pulled back on track, and by whom; where interpersonal exchanges are getting in the way, etc. The observer watches and takes careful notes on the meeting process, specifically the various transactions or exchanges that occur between members—not the substance of the discussions per se. The observer then presents and discusses his or her notes with the committee. The objective, of course, is for committee members, themselves, to identify counterproductive behaviors and attitudes so they can be eliminated. But the chair or facilitator must lead this examination.

Team Analysis

Team analysis is another group technique. Through this exercise, members discover what each brings, or potentially brings, to the committee. If a committee has been active for a period of time, but members seem not to be contributing, the chair points out that the group's members all bring different strengths to the committee. Dividing the committee into small groups, the chair then asks one member (A) of each small group to give another member (B) his or her subjective view of what strengths that member brings, or could bring, to the committee. Member B then does the same with member A. The large committee is then reconvened, and the chair asks if members would like to share their observations of the others. The subjects then get the opportunity to show where they agree or disagree with the other person's perception. While this technique can backfire badly, depending on the chemistry of the group, it can also succeed in loosening up and engaging individual members more productively in the committee's tasks.

However, psychological techniques like transaction analysis, team analysis, Lefties' *Johari Window* exercise (which engages committee members in a form of behavior self-analysis), or even "meeting as play" techniques (as in playing with ideas), are dangerous tools for the unskilled. Therefore, I do not recommend them except in unique situations. When a committee appears to be dysfunctional enough to require the use of techniques such as these, it is probably best for the chair to bring in an experienced, independent meeting facilitator to run the meetings.

Structural Modification

Of far more use to committees and committee leaders are structural modification techniques. As indicated earlier, committees work through meetings. As there are different kinds of committees (executive committees, creative/brainstorming committees, problem-solving committees), any kind of committee can decide to co-opt the structural characteristics, or meeting style, of any other kind of committee to address certain tasks.

For example, creative committees characteristically employ free-wheeling, loosely structured meetings, and use brainstorming as a technique for generating ideas. But any kind of committee could use brainstorming techniques to generate ideas.

Any committee might have the need for an *expert resource meeting,* in which it taps the advice of those individuals on the committee who are uncontested as the most knowledgeable, experienced, or expert on some particular aspect related to the committee's area of inquiry.

Information presentation meetings can be useful to any committee requiring knowledge of some aspect of their charge. Presentation meetings are usually structured, highly linear meetings at which someone presents information, which is followed by general discussion.

Training meetings might also be used when a committee needs "to learn" something as it deals with issues related to recommendations under consideration.

Subcommittees often use simple *problem-solving meetings* to efficiently address and execute tasks to be brought back to the larger committee. These meetings generally follow a series of steps in which:

(1) The problem or task is defined.
(2) Data and other pieces of information are assembled, examined, and discussed.
(3) Options are outlined.
(4) Criteria for evaluation of the options are determined.
(5) The options are analyzed.
(6) Conclusions and recommendations are made.

One of the most popular structural meeting style modifications used by committees today is the *interactive meeting.*

Interactive Meeting Techniques

The interactive meeting is a unique style of operation that, by its nature, requires the use of a facilitator assisted by a secretary/recorder. While not a new idea, the interactive meeting is a relatively modern style of committee operation. It is called "interactive" because power, as such, does not reside with the chair in an interactive meeting; each individual participant takes part on an equal basis with every other participant. The flow of the meeting is directed and managed by an independent, non-evaluating, neutral facilitator.

The Leadership Function

When a facilitator is used as meeting leader, he or she automatically takes over those responsibilities normally carried out by the chair. The facilitator uses the same fundamental techniques of meeting planning and organization as discussed above and throughout this book. In an interactive meeting, it is the facilitator's role to engage and involve all members of the committee in discussions; to protect each participant and his or her ideas from attack; and to eventually lead the committee to consensus—not, hopefully, just compromise—on the matters at hand. It is the facilitator's responsibility to organize and guide the committee's meeting(s) by calling on participants; clarifying points raised by participants in discussion; making certain that all participants and their views are respected; and summarizing ideas, as necessary, for the sake of greater clarity and for future action. An effective facilitator engages all participants in matters of agenda organization, and keeps all participants informed about what is happening and why in terms of the "process." Of critical importance is that the facilitator remain value neutral; it is not his or her role to judge the views of others, or to express a view of his or her own. The facilitator does not steer the committee to desired decisions, but guides the committee through the process of developing consensus on those matters to be addressed under the committee's charge.

The Recorder Function

To assist the committee and the facilitator, an independent recorder (independent committee secretary) is used to record committee output. This is a key role in the interactive meeting style. The recorder works at an easel or overhead projector at the central focal point of the meeting room. It is the recorder's job to write down, often using different colored pencils or crayons, the words that capture the essence of the ideas put forth by individual committee participants, as they happen, but usually without attribution. The pages can be torn off the easel, when full, and taped around the room so all can see. This written record, visible to all participants, becomes the committee's group memory. But this is more

than just recordkeeping. The process recognizes and respects all participant's ideas, and by retaining them, these pages can be reviewed or
reorganized by participants for future reference. The recorder is also a
neutral, non-judgmental servant of the committee, who does not interact
with the participants except to ask for clarification on what is being said
for purposes of accurate recording.

The Process

In practice, the interactive meeting is organized, planned, and set up
like any other kind of committee meeting. However, participants are
characteristically seated on chairs in a circular pattern; tables are not
used. As the facilitator is also part of the circle, the recorder is usually
located directly across the circle from the facilitator.

Once the chair has introduced committee members, related their
qualifications to each other, and focused the committee on the charge,
he or she introduces the facilitator. The facilitator then carries out the
process of centering the tasks relative to the charge, and begins to develop
the work plan with the committee. The process is basically one of
engagement.

The facilitator might begin with questions to the committee. "What do
we know, relative to this charge? What information do we have?" The
facilitator then goes around the circle or calls upon individuals as they
volunteer responses with the recorder taking down each participant's
contributions on a large paper tablet mounted on the easel. The next step
would most likely continue the process of inquiry, as the facilitator asks
"What information do we need?" The third question then follows: "How
can we find out what we need to know?" Again, as committee members
respond, the recorder notes their responses. These three questions will
usually outline the committee's work plan, as well as establish the tone
and working style of the interactive meeting; the facilitator leads with
questions; the committee members respond with information, concerns,
and responses to others' contributions.

After many more meetings, the facilitator will eventually begin to lead
the committee in discussions toward the objective of building consensus.
And here, something interesting very often occurs. The solutions (consensus decisions) of the group usually turn out to be better than the
individual solutions of most of the individual participants on the committee—often better than the best individual solution. This is the power
of consensus, as opposed to compromise or decisions made by individu-

als. But to achieve this, members must observe some simple rules of exchange throughout the consensus building process:

(1) Participants must not strive for agreement and harmony too early. It is best to cultivate and explore conflicting views.

(2) Participants must explain their own views, logically and clearly, but then listen and try to understand the views of others, rather than just debate and over-sell one position.

(3) Participants must help to seek win/win solutions. A consensus is not so much a compromise as a position at which everyone perceives they have either won something—not lost something important.

(4) Participants must articulate why they can support the consensus once it is finally reached. A consensus is a decision that every member can support in some way, and with reason.

Strengths of the Interactive Style

The strengths of the interactive meeting style are that objective, independent meeting management is provided in the person of the facilitator; that the chair is able to function as a full-fledged group member, and that high quality, consensus decisions can be more readily achieved because of the interactive technique's peculiar built-in dynamic. As pointed out by authors Doyle and Straus in their text on the interactive method:

> The Interactive Method functions like the automatic pilot on an airplane. If the meeting gets pushed off course the system of roles and relationships can correct itself automatically. If the facilitator steps out of line, the group members and [the chair] will push back. If the recorder begins to editorialize, the meeting participants will object. If the [chair] attacks group members or vice versa, the facilitator can intercede. The method is so simple that any group can understand the system and learn to run its own meetings effectively.[8]

The interactive meeting is a valuable technique for committee organization and management. It is one of many structural modifications committees and committee leaders can affect to make their meetings more productive. However, these are all just techniques; leadership is still the key.

---

[8]Doyle, Michael and Straus, David. *The New Interaction Method: How to Make Meetings Work.* New York: Jove Books, 1982, p. 87.

THE GOAL OF LEADERSHIP

The successful committee leader can be a chair or a facilitator. The effective leader has many styles and techniques at his or her disposal. And, there are many ways for the leader to draw effectively from all participants. But every successful committee leader must be a good organizer and planner, a careful listener, a director, a coordinator, a clarifier, a traffic police officer, a peacemaker, a challenger, a thoughtful host or hostess, an effective communicator, and ultimately a "packager" of ideas. To do all of these things with *style,* meaning with seemingly little obvious effort, as Somerset Maugham defined it, is to practice successfully the art of Committee.

Argyris, C. *Intervention Theory and Method.* Reading, MA.: Addison-Wesley, 1970.

Aronson, E. *The Social Animal.* San Francisco: W. H. Freeman, 1972.

Back, Kenneth and Kate. *Assertive at Work: A Practical Guide to Handling Awkward Situations.* New York: McGraw-Hill, 1982.

Bales, R. F. *Interaction Process Analysis.* Reading, MA: Addison-Wesley, 1950.

Berne, Eric. *Games People Play.* New York: Ballantine Books, 1964.

Bonner, H. *Group Dynamics: Principles and Applications.* New York: Ronald Press, 1959.

Bradford, Leland P. *Making Meetings Work: A Guide for Leaders and Group Members.* San Diego, Calif: University Associates, 1976.

Burke, P. Leadership Role Differentiation. In C. McClintock (ed.) *Experimental Social Psychology.* New York: Holt, Rinehart & Winston, 1972.

Cohen, Herb. *You Can Negotiate Anything.* New York: Bantam Books, 1982.

Crosbie, Paul V. *Interaction in Small Groups.* New York: Macmillan, 1975.

De Pree, Max. *Leadership Is an Art.* New York: Dell, 1989.

Doyle, Michael and Straus, David. *How to Make Meetings Work.* New York: Jove Books, 1982.

Drucker, Peter. *The Effective Executive.* New York: Harper & Row, 1969.

Fast, Julius. *Body Language.* New York: Pocket Books, 1981.

Fletcher, Winston. *Meetings: How to Manipulate Them and Make Them More Fun.* New York, New York: William Morrow, 1984.

Fordyce, Jack and Weil, Raymond. *Managing with People.* Menlo Park: Addison-Wesley, 1971.

Goffman, Erving. *Interaction Ritual: Essays in Face-to-Face Behavior.* New York: Pantheon, 1982.

Goodman, Paul and Assocs. *Designing Effective Work Groups.* San Francisco: Jossey-Bass, 1986.

Gordon, W. J. *Synectics.* New York: Harper & Row, 1961.

Gordon, Myron. *How To Plan & Conduct A Successful Meeting.* New York: Sterling Publishing Co., 1985.

Hackman, J. Richard, ed. *Groups That Work (And Those That Don't).* San Francisco: Jossey-Bass, 1990.

Hayes, Marion E. *Effective Meeting Skills.* Los Altos, CA: Crisp Publications, Inc., 1988.

Hersey, P. and Blanchard, K. *Management of Organizational Behavior: Utilizing Human Resources.* Englewood Cliffs, N.J.: Prentice Hall, 1977.

Hon, David. *Meetings That Matter.* New York: John Wiley & Sons, 1980.

Janis, Irving. *Victims of Groupthink.* Boston: Houghton Mifflin, 1972.

Jay, Antony. *Management and Machiavelli.* Kent, England: Hodder and Stoughton, 1967.

Johnson, David and Johnson, Frank. *Joining Together: Group Theory and Group Skills.* Englewood Cliffs, NJ.: Prentice Hall, 1985.

Katzenbach, Jon R. and Smith, Douglas. *The Wisdom of Teams.* Boston: Harvard Business School Press, 1993.

Kotter, John and Heskett, James. *Corporate Culture and Performance.* New York: Free Press, 1992.

Locke, Michael. *How to Run Committees and Meetings.* London: Macmillan, 1980.

Mann, Dale. *The Politics of Administrative Representation.* Lexington, MA: D. C. Heath & Co., 1976.

Marrow, A. *Making Management Human.* New York: McGraw-Hill, 1957.

Maslow, A. H. *Motivation and Personality.* New York: Harper & Row, 1954.

McDavid, J. and Harari, H. *Social Psychology: Individuals,Groups, Societies.* New York: Harper & Row, 1968.

McGregor, D. *The Human Side of Enterprise.* New York: McGraw-Hill, 1967.

Milfes, Matthew. *Learning to Work in Groups.* New York: Teachers College Press, 1969.

Patton, R. and Griffin, K. *Problem Solving Group Interaction.* New York: Harper & Row, 1973.

Phillips, Gerald M. *Communication and the Small Group.* Indianapolis: Bobbs Merrill, 1966.

Rawlinson, J. Geoffrey. *Creative Thinking and Brainstorming.* New York: John Wiley & Sons, Halsted Press, 1981.

Peters, Tom. *Thriving on Chaos.* New York: Alfred A. Knopf, 1987.

Reeves, Elton T. *The Dynamics of Group Behavior.* New York: American Management Association, 1970.

Robert, General Henry M. Guide and Commentary by Rachel Vixman. *Rules of Order.* New York: Jove Publications, 1977.

Sheflen, Albert E. *Body Language and the Social Order.* Englewood Cliffs, N.J. Prentice-Hall, Spectrum Books, 1973.

Simon, H. *Administrative Behavior: A Study of Decision-Making Processes in Administrative Organization.* New York: Free Press, 1976.

Steiner, Ivan D. *Group Process and Productivity.* New York: Academic Press, 1972.

Weisbord, Marvin. *Productive Workplaces.* San Francisco: Jossey-Bass, 1989.

ROBERT K. LABER chaired his first formal committee more than twenty-seven years ago—as an Arts Director in the Boston area. He has been working in education administration and leading committees ever since—first as an Assistant to the Superintendent on Long Island, and since the early 1980s, as an Assistant Superintendent for the Darien, Connecticut Public Schools. Bob holds degrees from Oberlin and Yale. He studied curriculum development at Harvard and earned his Doctorate (Ed.D.) in Education Administration from Teachers College, Columbia University in 1982. His primary areas of interest are organizational behavior, curriculum and testing, and organizational planning. Bob is an educational management consultant with Columbia Associates of Danbury, Connecticut and New York City. He is currently a member of the Educational Records Bureau Board of Advisors, and serves on the Connecticut State Education Department Advisory Council on Professional Certification. Bob has published numerous articles on subjects as diverse as planning, testing and assessment; developmental psychology and motivation; and curriculum development studies in most academic curriculum areas. From 1989–1994 he wrote on music and musicians for *Instrumentalist* and *Clavier* magazines. Over his past twenty-seven years, as a district level administrator and consultant, Laber has chaired hundreds of effective committees, and shown others how to use them more productively.